Conducting the J2EE Job Inte

IT Manager Guide for J2EE with Inte

Jeffrey M. Hunter

I dedicate this book to my wife Melody and our son Alex whose love and support made this book possible.

--- Jeff Hunter

Conducting the J2EE Job Interview
IT Manager Guide for J2EE with Interview Questions

By Jeffrey M. Hunter

Copyright © 2004 by Rampant TechPress. All rights reserved.

Printed in the United States of America.

Published by Rampant TechPress, Kittrell, North Carolina, USA

IT Job Interview Series: Book #6

Series Editor: Don Burleson

Editors: Janet Burleson, John Lavender, and Linda Webb

Production Editor: Teri Wade

Cover Design: Janet Burleson

Printing History:

April 2004 for First Printing, January 2007 for Second Printing

Java, J2EE, J2SE, J2ME, and all Java-based marks are trademarks or registered trademarks of Sun Microsystems Corporation. *IT Job Interview* is a registered Trademark of Rampant TechPress.

ISBN: 0-9744355-9-7
ISBN-13: 978-0-9744355-9-6

Library of Congress Control Number: 2004101893

Table of Contents

Using the Online Code Depot

Your purchase of this book provides you with complete access to the online code depot that contains the sample questions and answers.

All of the job questions in this book are located at the following URL:

rampant.cc/job_j2ee.htm

All of the sample tests and questions in this book will be available for download, ready to use for your next interview.

If you need technical assistance in downloading or accessing the scripts, please contact Rampant TechPress at info@rampant.cc.

Get the Advanced Oracle Monitoring and Tuning Script Collection

The complete Oracle script collection from Mike Ault.

Packed with over 600 ready-to-use Oracle scripts, this is the definitive collection for every Oracle professional DBA.

It would take many years to develop these scripts from scratch, making this download the best value in the Oracle industry.

It's only $49.95 (only pennies per script!)

To buy for immediate download, go to
www.rampant.cc/aultcode.htm

Conventions Used in this Book

It is critical for any technical publication to follow rigorous standards and employ consistent punctuation conventions to make the text easy to read.

However, this is not an easy task. Within Java and J2EE there are many types of notations that can confuse a reader. Some Java technologies, such as J2SE, J2SE SDK, and J2EE are always spelled in CAPITAL letters, while Java parameters and procedures have varying naming conventions in the Java documentation. It is also important to remember that many Java commands are case sensitive, and are always left in their original executable form, and never altered with italics or capitalization.

Hence, all Rampant TechPress books follow these conventions:

Source Code – Anything that might appear in a Java or J2EE program, including code snippets, keywords, method names, variables names, class names, and interface names will use a `monospaced font`.

New Terms – An *Italics font* will be used for all new terms, book titles and for emphasis.

Parameters and Placeholders – A *lowercase italics font* will be used to identify any command-line parameters or placeholders required by the user.

Commands, Java and J2EE Programs – A `**bold monospaced font**` will be used to identify Java and J2EE binaries or command-line applications that will need to be typed by the user.

Products – All products that are known to the author are capitalized according to the vendor specifications (IBM, DBXray, Sun Microsystems, etc). All names known by Rampant TechPress to be trademark names appear in this text

---

as initial caps. References to UNIX are always made in uppercase.

Acknowledgements

This type of highly technical reference book requires the dedicated efforts of many people. Even though I am the author, my work ends when I deliver the content. After each chapter is delivered, several Java programmers and J2EE developers carefully review and correct the technical content. After the technical review, experienced copy editors polish the grammar and syntax. The finished work is then reviewed as page proofs and turned over to the production manager, who arranges the creation of the online code depot and manages the cover art, printing distribution, and warehousing.

In short, the author played a small role in the development of this book, and I need to thank and acknowledge everyone who helped bring this book to fruition:

Don Burleson, for asking me to write a book on this subject. Don has been an excellent source of motivation throughout my research and writing. Compiling this book has been a great opportunity in many ways, including enriching my knowledge of the Java language and the role it now plays in our industry.

Janet Burleson, for the production management, including the coordination of the cover art, page proofing, printing, and distribution.

John Garmany, for his help in the production of the page proofs.

JohnLavender, for his assistance with the web site, and for creating the code depot and the online shopping cart for this book.

With my sincerest thanks,

Jeffrey M. Hunter

Preface

After interviewing countless candidates for Java and J2EE related positions, I am aware that it is getting harder to locate and retain qualified J2EE professionals. You must cull the best fit from hundreds of resumes. Success depends upon knowing exactly which skills you need, and verifying that each candidate possesses acceptable levels of those skills.

That's where this book can help you. For both the new IT manager and the seasoned VP, the levels within the position of a J2EE professional will be explained to illustrate screening and interview techniques. In particular, I will define the differences between a J2EE architect and a J2EE developer. Some common misconceptions will be clarified about the J2EE position and tips will be provided on how to interview a candidate for this type of position.

Large numbers of J2EE neophytes are obtaining J2EE certification through the Sun Certified Web Component Developer (SCWCD), Sun Certified Business Component Developer (SCBCD), and Sun Certified Enterprise Architect (SCEA) program. This overabundance of Sun Certified J2EE developers makes it more important than ever to evaluate every candidate's experience and working knowledge of the Java language and the J2EE software platform.

Few IT managers, especially in smaller companies, have extensive formal training in interviewing and hiring techniques. Most interviewers' primary full-time responsibility will lie elsewhere. It is a fact that most IT managers do not even have a clear idea of the skills and personal characteristics their candidate should possess, much less an effective process for screening potential employees. Yet, nothing is more crucial to the success of the organization than doing everything possible to insure that the selected candidate is the best fit for the available position.

This book will provide effective techniques for finding committed employees who are able to function at a high level on the job. By eliminating guesswork, and rejecting the random hit-or-miss approach that is based on the instincts of the interviewer and little else, the employer can hire promising candidates with the confidence that the odds are stacked in his favor.

To help find, hire, and retain suitable J2EE professionals, background evaluation tips will be provided for identifying the best candidates. For the technical interview, sample questions and answers are also provided. A non-technical evaluation section is provided to help determine whether the candidate's personality is a good match for the organization and able to integrate seamlessly with your shop's particular culture.

Of course, there is no magic formula for determining if a candidate can perform properly, and no single screening test to ensure that you will properly evaluate a candidate's ability. However, if the employer and candidate are properly prepared, then filling the position successfully becomes less of a risk.

It is my hope that this book will become an indispensable tool for identifying, interviewing, and hiring top-notch J2EE professionals.

Conducting the J2EE Job Interview

The J2EE Developer Evaluation

Introduction

Since its official debut by Sun Microsystems in 1995, Java has matured from a tool that makes Applets, to an enterprise development environment able to support today's most mission critical applications. With its promise of platform independence, reliable security, and robust support for distributed network environments, companies of all types are embracing and adopting the J2EE software platform for developing their next generation IT applications. A survey performed in the year 2000 revealed more than 40% of Fortune 500 companies use Java. In the year 2003, this number has risen to well over 85% and continues to grow.

One of the results of the popularity of the J2EE platform is an ever increasing demand for top-notch J2EE professionals. However, culling experienced J2EE talent is difficult given the brief existence of the of J2EE vendors in the marketplace. As more companies continue to adopt the J2EE platform into their business, the demand for skilled J2EE professionals becomes vital to the success of the organization. However, this mushrooming need for J2EE developers and architects has created a vastly disparate job pool. Job skills range from software engineers with PhDs in Information Systems from top U.S. universities and 20 years' experience, to semi-literate J2EE developer trainees with 90 days' experience.

The result of the explosive growth of the Java industry is a two-tiered job market. Many top-rated universities teach Java and the J2EE software platform as part of their undergraduate CS or IT curriculum and produce candidates for career tracks in large corporations. At the same time, trade schools and community colleges produce hundreds of thousands of Java programmers and J2EE developers. No matter what the economic climate, large corporations actively recruit their entry-level talent for their mission-critical systems development from prestigious universities.

Written with the IT manager in mind, this book provides useful insight into the characteristics that make a successful J2EE professional job candidate.

J2EE Architect vs. J2EE Developer

As stated earlier, this book is about how to screen and interview potential candidates for a position as a J2EE professional. But what is a J2EE professional? What are the different levels within the position of a J2EE professional? In general, there are two types of J2EE professionals; the J2EE Architect and the J2EE Developer.

A J2EE developer is that person or persons on a project responsible for most of the coding using the J2EE software platform. The position of a J2EE developer will require significant knowledge of all J2EE components (Servlets, JSPs, and EJBs) and services (JDBC, JMS, JTA, etc.). The J2EE developer will also need to have a firm understanding of how to use version control systems, IDE, build tools, and working with UML diagrams. These developers will often get their direction from the J2EE architect of the project.

The J2EE Architect, on the other hand, is responsible for visualizing the behavior of the system as a whole. An architect is the one who creates the blueprint for the entire system. He or she defines the way in which the different elements and components of the system work together. The J2EE Architect commonly leads the development team to ensure the designers, programmers, and developers build the system according to the architecture.

Some of the common characteristics of a J2EE Architect is someone well-rounded, very experienced, able to make difficult decisions when required, educated, communicates well with others, an excellent leader, and someone who has a solid working knowledge of the business and problem domains.

Preparing the J2EE Professional Job Offering

One of the points that I repeatedly make is that top-notch J2EE professionals are hard to find and well compensated, while mediocre Java/J2EE developers are easy to find and hire.

On the high end, J2EE Enterprise Architects with over 10 years experience and graduate degrees typically command salaries ranging from $78,000 to $101,000 per year, depending on geographical location. For Principle Software Engineering consultants with strong Java and J2EE experience and a broad exposure in mission-critical areas, the sky is the limit. Certification also plays a critical role in determining salaries. On average, Sun Certified Java Programmers make approximately $78,000 a year while Sun Certified Developers make an average yearly salary of $84,500.

The first step in hiring a J2EE professional is determining the level of skill you require and preparing an incentive package. If your IT environment is mission-critical, then a seasoned J2EE professional with at least 5 years of experience is your safest choice. However, candidates with high skill levels and many years of experience often require incentives to abandon their employers.

Preparing the Incentive Package

If you want a top-notch Senior J2EE Enterprise Architect, you may be surprised to find them in short supply, even in a down job market. While every manager knows that salary alone cannot guarantee employee loyalty, there are a host of techniques used by IT management to attract and retain top-notch J2EE professionals.

J2EE professionals like the latest hardware and software!

In addition to a competitive salary, some of the techniques used to entice potential candidates include:

💻 **The Code Depot User ID = reader, Password = alex**

Flex time - Burnout can be a real problem among IT professionals who must typically work evenings, weekends and holidays to stay caught up with many demanding and sometimes conflicting project tasks. Many companies offer formal comp-time policies or institute a four-day workweek, allowing those employees to work four, 10-hour days per week.

Telecommuting - Many J2EE professionals are allowed to work at home and only visit the office once per week for important face-to-face meetings.

Golden handcuffs - Because a high base salary does not always reduce attrition, many IT managers use yearly bonuses to retain employees. Golden handcuffs may take the form of a Management by Objective (MBO) structure, whereby the J2EE professional receives a substantial annual bonus for meeting management expectations. Some companies implement golden handcuffs by paying the employee a huge signing bonus (often up to $50,000) and requiring the employee to return the bonus if he or she leaves the company in less than three years. However, don't be surprised to find that some competing companies will reimburse the J2EE professional to repay a retention bonus.

Fancy job titles - Because J2EE professionals command high salaries, many are given honorary job titles other than simply Java Programmer. These include Business Analyst, Programmer Analyst, Enterprise Architect, and Systems Engineer. Other J2EE titles include Vice President of

---

Software Engineering, Chief Technologist, and the new job title (used by Bill Gates), Chief Software Architect.

Specialized training - J2EE professionals are commonly rewarded by being allowed to attend conferences and training classes. An entire industry is built around these large Java events. For example, every year thousands of Java developers gather for one week in San Francisco for the JavaOne^{SM} conference. Here, great minds in Java and J2EE get together to celebrate Java technology, innovation, community and education. On June 10th 2003 Sun Microsystems also launched JavaOne Online for those wishing the JavaOne^{SM} conference could be held all year long. JavaOne Online was designed to portray the spirit of the physical JavaOne conference and offer it to Java developers worldwide. Other popular conferences amongst Java and J2EE developers are:

- Software Development Conference and Expo
- Colorado Software Summit – Java™ and XML Programming Conference
- Conference on the Principles and Practice of Programming in Java™ in Kilkenny City, Ireland
- Premier European Developer Conference on Java™ Technology and Object-Oriented Software Engineering (JAOO).
- The Geek Cruise Line offers technical conferences on hot topics like Java, Oracle, Perl combined with an ocean cruise. An Eastern Cruise called Java Jam 4 will be offered in January 2004.

Defining the Required Job Skills

A number of candidates mistakenly believe that the job of the J2EE professional is purely technical. In reality, the J2EE professional must be efficient and knowledgeable in all areas of IT, because he or she often has the ultimate responsibility for overall design, implementation, and user acceptance of the final system. Excellent interpersonal skills and communicative abilities are required, as well as technical skills in all phases of the software development lifecycle.

Remember, knowledge of Java and the J2EE framework is not enough. An understanding of operating systems and computer-science theory is imperative as well. That is why employers like to hire J2EE professionals who also have a background in computer science, information systems, or business administration.

It is also critical to remember that Java and J2EE certification tells employers only that the job candidate successfully passed a certification test on the technical aspects of the Java language and J2EE platform. In the real world, Java certification is just one of many criteria used to evaluate a J2EE professional job candidate. Other criteria include the following:

Excellent Communication Skills — As one of the key stakeholders in any new systems development, the J2EE professional must possess exceptional communication skills. Effective communication skills not only include speaking but strong proficiencies in reading and writing as well.

In many application development shops, it is the responsibility of the J2EE architect to communicate technical and sometimes highly complex information to top-level management and other public groups. As the central technical guru, he or she must be able to explain concepts clearly in terms of the big picture. The audience may consist of all stakeholders including management, users, DBAs, and other developers participating in strategic planning and architectural reviews.

Formal Education – Many employers require J2EE professionals to have a bachelor's degree in Computer Science or Information Systems. For advanced positions such as a Principle Software Architect or Enterprise Development Architect, many employers prefer a master's degree in computer science or a master's in business administration (MBA).

Real-World Experience - This requirement is the catch-22 for newbie's who possess only a Sun Java Certification. A common complaint of people who have Java/J2EE Certification but no job experience is that they cannot get experience without the certification, and they cannot get a job without experience. This is especially true in a tight job market.

Problem Solving Abilities - A successful candidate should also have the ability to translate raw concepts from vague design specs and paper-based storyboards through prototypes all the way to a finished product. When analyzing problems in development, experienced J2EE professionals are able to recommend and implement effective solutions throughout all phases of development. They possess a deep-seated desire to develop innovative learning and teaching products and show profound capabilities for learning new topics. As an expert in problem solving and organizational skills, a good candidate will possess the ability to evaluate information while making efficient architectural and design decisions.

Knowledge of Object Oriented Design Theory - In addition to mastering the technical details required for the Sun Java Certification exams, the successful J2EE professional must have a strong understanding of object oriented design methodologies. This includes intimate knowledge of object-oriented design theory, object-oriented application design,

CRC methods, design patterns as well as object-oriented modeling with Unified Modeling Language (UML).

Basic IT Skills

Because the J2EE professional is often called upon to perform critical projects in the IT department, a broad background is often desirable. Much of this basic IT knowledge is taught in academic Computer Science and Information Technology programs. Non-Java programming and non-J2EE development job skills include:

System Analysis & Design – Many J2EE professionals must take an active role in the analysis and design of new application systems. Hence, knowledge of relational databases, data flow diagrams, CASE tools, Entity-relation modeling and design techniques enhance the J2EE candidates' scope of ability.

Database Design – Depending on the application being designed, many J2EE professionals' jobs require knowledge of some database theory, STAR schema design, and data modeling techniques.

Data/Application Security Principles – An understanding of database and application security, including role-based security, is useful especially for US Government positions.

XML and Web Services – Knowledge of XML and Web Services (UDDI, SOAP, ebXML, WDSL) is essential when designing distributed enterprise systems.

Change Control Management – In many cases the J2EE professional will be responsible for utilizing version control and code sharing systems to insure that changes to the production code base are properly coordinated. Knowledge of third-party change control tools, such as the UNIX Source Code Control System (SCCS), CVS, Oracle SCM, or Continuus is essential.

Now that we have an understanding of some of the required skills, let's talk about Java and J2EE certification. The Sun Java Certified Professional exams identify candidates who have mastered specific technical areas within the Java programming language and J2EE application framework. However, as interviewers frequently discover, possession of these certificates provides no guarantee that a candidate has real Java or J2EE development expertise.

Sun Certified J2EE Developers and Architects

Lured by the promise of a large paycheck, thousands of ordinary people from every walk of life have managed to complete "Java and J2EE boot camps" that teach them how to pass the Sun Certified Java and J2EE exams. Although possessing a certification from Sun Microsystems as either a Java Programmer/Developer or a Java Enterprise Architect, these certified professionals are applying for and obtaining jobs in application development shops without the appropriate IT background. If this is possible and happening in today's job market, then what is the value of a certification in Java?

The Value of Java and J2EE Certification

Starting with the obvious question, what is the value of Java and J2EE Certification? Considering that at the time of publication, these Certification Exams cost $150 each and factoring in the cost of books, classes, and other study materials, certification is a sizable investment. However, the potential rewards can make that investment worthwhile.

Here's the catch – Java and J2EE Certification alone is not a guarantee that anyone will find employment in application development. Obtaining a Java/J2EE Certification is just one of the credentials valued by prospective employers. Certification allows developers and architects to attest to their knowledge of Java and J2EE by alluding to their certification credentials.

All together, there are five Java certifications offered by Sun Microsystems that are divided up into two major technology areas: Java 2 Platform, Standard Edition (J2SE) and the Java 2 Platform, Enterprise Edition (J2EE). The follow section provides a brief description of all five Java certifications within the J2SE and J2EE technology areas:

Java 2 Platform, Standard Edition (J2SE)

Sun Certified Programmer for the Java 2 Platform

This certification is for programmers interested in demonstrating proficiency in the fundamentals of the Java programming language including Objects and Classes, Modifiers, Flow Control, Operators and Assignments, Exceptions, I/O, Collections and Maps, Inner Classes, Threads, and use of the java.lang and java.util packages.

Sun Certified Developer for Java 2 Platform

This certification is designed for programmers and developers who already have a basic understanding of the basic structure and syntax of the Java programming language. Candidates attempting this performance-based certification need to demonstrate advanced proficiency in developing complex, production-level applications using J2SE. In order to pass the Sun Certified Developer exam, candidates should possess strong skills with Swing Components and Events, Layout Managers, Networking with Sockets and RMI, utilizing Threads with NIO and Swing, and knowledge with Relational Database Technology utilizing JDBC.

Obtaining certification as a Sun Certified Developer consists of two elements: a programming assignment and an essay exam, and requires Sun Certified Programmer for Java 2 Platform (any edition) status.

Java 2 Platform, Enterprise Edition (J2EE)

Sun Certified Web Component Developer for the Java 2 Platform, Enterprise Edition

This certification is for programmers developing Java Web Applications. Achieving this certification demands an in-depth knowledge with developing applications using JavaServer Pages (JSP) and servlet technologies used to present Web services and dynamic Web content using J2EE. The candidate should also have strong skills with Servlet Session Management, Thread Safety with Servlets, Web Application Security, Web Application Deployment, Customize Tag Libraries and Design Patterns.

Obtaining a certification as a Web Component Developer entails passing one exam and also requires Sun Certified Programmer for Java 2 Platform (any edition) status.

Sun Certified Business Component Developer for the Java 2 Platform, Enterprise Edition

Designed for Java developers specializing in leveraging the J2EE platform by developing server-side components that encapsulate the business logic of an application. This certification concentrates on testing a candidate's knowledge of designing, coding, testing, deploying, and integrating Enterprise Java Beans (EJB) applications.

Obtaining a certification as a Business Component Developer for Java entails passing one exam and also requires Sun Certified Programmer for Java 2 Platform (any edition) status.

Sun Certified Enterprise Architect for the Java 2 Platform, Enterprise Edition

For enterprise architects responsible for architecting and designing J2EE compliant applications, this certification tests a candidate's skill in producing applications that are scalable, flexible and highly secure. A candidate should be exceedingly familiar with resolving complex design issues and the technologies offered in the Java 2 Platform, Enterprise Edition used to build Java-based enterprise applications

Obtaining a certification as an Enterprise Architect for Java consists of three elements: a knowledge-based multiple-choice exam, an assignment and essay exam.

Training for Certification

The Sun Java Certification program has evolved into a structured array of exams and certifications, and the number of exams will only continue to evolve as new functionality is added to the J2EE platform. This popularity in Java and J2EE certification has created a new market for classes and books dedicated to helping candidates pass the exams. Although someone's knowledge of the J2EE platform should suffice in successfully passing any of the exams, candidates often purchase books that contain practice exams. Often these practice exams provide the candidate with a general feel for the testing environment and whether or not they may be ready for the actual exam.

Both J2EE professionals and hiring managers can use the certifications as a gauge of competence, but real-world experience must never be discounted. While certification in Java and J2EE is not a complete measure of a person's skills, it does demonstrate a modicum of talent and provides a method for those with degrees in Computer Science of Business Administration to enter the Java and J2EE job field.

For a J2EE candidate, depth of knowledge in object-oriented programming design, problem solving techniques, years of experience is far more important than their ability to pass the Sun Certified Java exams. Employers are recognizing the pitfalls of hiring people based solely upon Java and J2EE certification.

Characteristics of the J2EE Professional

While many application development shops have hundreds of technology workers, retention efforts are normally focused on seasoned J2EE professionals, whose knowledge of the company's application systems is not easily transferred to replacements.

In many development shops, the J2EE professional may serve many roles. In addition to traditional responsibilities found in software engineering, the J2EE professional is often called upon to serve as a system architect, functional lead, or an Informaticist (a functional IT professional who possesses an MS in computer science and is also trained in professional areas, such as medicine, business management or accounting), a database administrator, or a system administrator.

The following attributes are signs of a first rate J2EE professional:

Has earned at least one professional degree or certification - Possessing a degree such as MD, JD, MBA, MSEE, or CPA, in addition to an undergraduate degree, makes an employee a valuable asset, one difficult to replace in the open job market.

Has graduated from a competitive university - J2EE professionals must be self-starting and highly motivated to be effective, and this is often indicated by entrance to competitive universities with rigorous admission standards. These schools include most Ivy League schools, especially MIT, and universities with stellar reputations in Information Systems such as Purdue, the University of Texas, the University of California at Los Angeles, the University of San Diego, and the University of California at Berkeley.

Is trained in a special skill - J2EE professionals with specialized, difficult-to-find training are often in high demand. Examples of specialized skills are ERP Systems (Oracle 11i, SAP, BaaN), Relational Database Technologies (Oracle, MySQL, PostGress), and J2EE Software Platforms (Oracle9iAS, BEA WebLogic, IBM WebSphere).

Active in the Java community - Many good J2EE professionals participate in local user groups, present techniques, and publish in many of the Java and J2EE related periodicals.

Is recognized as a Java and J2EE expert - A sure sign of a top-notch J2EE professional is someone who gets in front of audiences by publishing a book, writing a magazine article, or appearing as a conference speaker.

Possesses irreplaceable knowledge of an institution's enterprise systems - If the employee serves in a mission-critical developer role, such as Chief Architect or Principal Software Engineer, a vacuum in the Application Development Department may be created by that employee's departure.

Sample Job Sheet for a Senior J2EE Architect

Applicants for any J2EE professional position are expected to meet all the requirements in mission-critical areas, including education, experience, certification, writing credits, personal characteristics and legal standing. Here is an example job requirement sheet for the position of Senior J2EE Architect:

Sample J2EE Job Sheet

These are the minimum job requirements for the position of Senior J2EE Architect. The HR department will pre-screen all candidates for the following job skills and experience.

Education

Persons with Bachelor's, Masters Degrees, and Ivy League graduates are desired. At a minimum, the candidate is expected to possess a four-year degree from a fully-accredited university in a discipline such as Computer Science, Software Engineering, BA or MBA in Information Systems (from an AACSB accredited university), or Engineering (electrical, mechanical, or chemical).

Work Experience

The candidate should have five or more years programming in object-oriented Java, two or more years programming with the Java 2 Enterprise Edition platform and five or more years experience with Unix/Linux system environments.

Sun Java / J2EE Certification

The candidate must have earned the following certifications through Sun Microsystems within the last two years:
Sun Java Programmer Certification
Sun Java Developer Certification
Sun Java 2 Enterprise Edition Web Component Developer
Sun Java 2 Enterprise Architect

Publishing and Research

The candidate should show demonstrable interest in publishing Java and J2EE research as evidenced by participating in user groups and publishing of articles, books and columns. These include:

Books. Proposals for publication may be submitted to Java or J2EE technical books or any other recognized academic publication company.

Articles for academic journals. For example, the Journal of the IEEE, Management Science, Journal of Management Information Systems and the Journal of Systems & Software.

Conference papers. Writing papers and presenting at conferences such as Java World, JAOO, and Colorado Software Summit.

Articles in trade publications. Writing an article for a trade publication such as Java Developer's Journal, JAVA Pro, Java World, or Dr. Dobbs Journal.

Personal Integrity

This position requires designing and coding distributed, mission-critical applications and accessing confidential data. All candidates are required to sign a waiver to disclose personal information.

The candidate must have no history of acts of moral turpitude, drug use, dishonesty, lying, cheating, or theft.

USA Citizenship

We are unable to sponsor H1-B foreign consultants. Therefore, candidates must provide proof of US citizenship.

Additional Specialized Skills

The following specialized skills are desired:

- Bachelor's or Masters degree from a major university.

- An active US Secret, Top secret or Q-level security clearance.

- Working knowledge of Oracle9iAS Containers for J2EE (OC4J).

- Use Case design.

- Understands the lifecycle of enterprise application development (requirement till production) and understands different development processes (XP and RUP, waterfall, spiral, etc.).

- Understand how to create scalable and highly available

application at the database, application server and messaging layers (using load balancing and clustering).

- Proficient in database performance tuning (especially with Oracle).

- Skilled in how clustering and load balancing works.

- Knowledge with how messaging (Oracle Advanced Queuing or MQSeries) might fit in distributed architecture.

- Human Resource Systems from Oracle11i, SAP, or PeopleSoft.

- Strong knowledge in UNIX scripting languages including KSH and BASH

As shown above, positions as J2EE professionals have requirements that vary widely, and it is up to the IT manager to choose those qualities that best suit the position.

Conclusion

This chapter has been concerned with identifying the job requirements of a skilled and experienced J2EE candidate and preparing an incentive package. Next, let's take a look at how to evaluate the J2EE professional for specific job skills.

The Successful
J2EE Professional

Quality

Determining the quality of a successful candidate starts with evaluating the résumé. This is such a critical part of the selection process. Given a tight job market, it is not uncommon for HR and IT management to receive hundreds of résumés. It is critical for HR and IT management to understand how to fairly and efficiently pre-screen applicants and only forward qualified individuals to the hiring manager for a detailed interview. Let's start by looking at techniques for evaluating the job history of a J2EE professional.

A good Java programmer will demonstrate persistence!

Evaluating Employment History

Without question, the evaluation of a J2EE professional's work history is the single most critical factor in résumé screening. In most cases, candidates without a significant amount of work history will spend an excessive amount of time learning their jobs, while a higher paid, experienced candidate may be a better overall value for the hiring company.

Not all J2EE development experience is equal. Many demanding application development shops provide exceptional training and experience, while others provide only glancing exposure to the J2EE application environment.

When evaluating the work experience of a J2EE professional candidate, the following factors should be considered:

Job role – J2EE candidates who have had positions of responsibility in areas of design and architecture decisions are often more qualified than those candidates for whom the Java and J2EE development skills were a part-time duty.

Employer-sponsored Java and J2EE education – Within many large corporations, IT employees are encouraged and in some cases required to participate in yearly training events in order to keep their skill sets current. One good indicator of an employer's quality is to investigate how much on-the-job education is available to their employees. Employer-sponsored, yearly Java training and participation in Java groups and conferences (JavaOne^{SM}, JAOO) are indications of a good background for a J2EE professional.

Fraudulent Work History

In the soft market of the early twenty-first century, it is not uncommon for a desperate J2EE professional job applicant to forge a work history with a defunct dot-com. The desperate applicant hopes that this fraud will not be detected. This phenomenon presents the IT manager with a unique challenge in verifying employment history with a company that no longer exists or contacting job references who cannot speak English.

In many cases, the HR staff strongly discounts résumés where the employment and educational history cannot be completely verified. Many departments, frustrated with confirming overseas employment histories, never forward these types of résumés to the IT manager.

Evaluating Personal Integrity

It is always a good idea to perform a background check, which is easily obtained via national services. Many companies require that a candidate not have any criminal convictions, except minor traffic violations. In some cases, a routine background check can reveal arrests and acts of moral turpitude.

A J2EE professional's ongoing responsibilities often include designing and coding mission-critical and distributed application components with confidential data. Therefore, some companies require that all applicants for the position of Java programmer or J2EE developer to demonstrate the highest degree of personal and moral integrity.

In addition, acts of moral turpitude, such as a history of drug use, dishonesty, lying, cheating, or theft may be grounds for immediate rejection. In some companies, all applicants are expected to sign a waiver to disclose personal information and are asked to submit to a polygraph exam.

Evaluating Academic History

While formal education is not always a predictor of success as a J2EE professional, there can be no doubt that job candidates with advanced degrees from respected universities possess both the high intelligence and persistence needed in a top-notch working professional

The Quality of Education

When evaluating the educational background of job candidates, it is important to remember that not all colleges are created equal. Many IT managers tend to select candidates from top tier colleges and universities because they rely on the universities to do the prescreening for them.

For example, an IT professional who has been able to enroll in a top tier university clearly demonstrates high achievement, high intelligence, and a very strong work ethic. At the other end of the spectrum, there are many IT candidates who have attended vocational schools, night schools, and non-accredited universities to receive bachelor's degrees in nontraditional study areas. In many cases, these IT professionals lack the necessary technical and communicational skills required to succeed in the IT industry.

The type of degree is also a factor in the suitability of the IT candidate. For example, an ABS or MS in Computer Science generally requires the IT job candidate to have a very strong theoretical background in mathematics and physics. Those with formal degrees in computer science tend to gravitate toward software engineering and software development fields that require in-depth knowledge about lower-level components in computer systems.

On the other hand, we see BS and Master's degrees in Information Systems. Those degrees offered by accredited business colleges (accredited by the American Assembly of Collegiate Business Schools, AACBS) tend to strike a balance between IT programming skills and business skills. The information systems degree candidate will have a background in systems analysis and design, as well as familiarity with functional program development for specific business processes.

Unlike computer science majors, information systems majors will have a background in accounting, finance, marketing, economics, and other areas of business administration that equip them to solve business problems.

Many IT shops save time by letting universities pre-screen Java and J2EE candidates. For example, MIT carefully screens grades and achievement, and this pre-screening by the university allows companies to choose professionals with increased confidence in the candidate's required skills.

The type of job to be filled may determine the academic history required. For example, a J2EE developer may not require a four-year degree, while a lead J2EE architect for a large corporation may require a Master's degree from a respected university.

Note: This section is based upon the author's experience in evaluating J2EE professionals and the HR policies of large application development shops. This section is in no way meant to discredit those J2EE job applicants without the benefit of a college education.

Rating College Education

Many shops have an HR professional evaluate education, while other IT managers take it upon themselves to evaluate the technical quality of the J2EE professional candidate's formal education. Fortunately, sources for rating colleges and universities can be found online. Many large corporations require that the job candidate's degree must be from a university possessing a first-tier or second-tier rating by US News & World Report's "America's Best Colleges" or degrees from exceptional universities (as listed in the Gourman Report).

Some computer professionals are insecure about their vocabulary

Of course, not all jobs as a J2EE professional require a college degree. For lower-level J2EE web development positions, the formal academic requirements are less challenging, but the lead J2EE enterprise architect for a large corporation must possess high intelligence, superb communications skills, and the drive and persistence that is most commonly associated with someone who has taken the time to invest in a quality education.

College Major and Job Suitability

There is a great deal of debate about what academic majors, if any, are the best indicators of success in the position of a J2EE professional. However, it is well documented that different majors attract students with varying abilities. The following list describes some indicators used in large corporations for assessing the relative value of different college majors:

Engineers - Engineers tend to make great J2EE architects, especially those with degrees in Electrical Engineering (EE). An engineering curriculum teaches logical thinking, algorithm design, and data structure theory that makes it easy for the engineer to quickly learn the concepts of object oriented programming with Java and J2EE. However, while engineers have unimpeachable technical skills, their oral and written communication skills are often lacking. Therefore, IT managers should pay careful attention to communication skills when interviewing J2EE applicants with engineering degrees.

Business Majors - Business majors make excellent J2EE developers because of their training in finance, accounting, marketing, and other business processes. Many business schools also require matriculated students to take several courses in Information Technology. Not all college business schools are equal, though. When screening a J2EE job applicant with a business major, time should be taken to insure that the degree is from a business school accredited by the American Assembly of Collegiate Business Schools (AACSB). There are many fly-by-night business schools, and their depth of training may be vastly different.

Computer Science Majors - Computer scientists typically receive four years of extensive technical training, and are ideal candidates for the role of jobs requiring in-depth technical ability. However, like the engineers, many computer scientists have sub-standard communications skills.

Music Majors - For many years, IBM recruited from the ranks of college musicians because hiring managers found that musicians possessed an ability in logical thinking that made them ideal candidates for IT skill training.

Math Majors - Math majors tend to possess excellent logical thinking skills and often possess a background in Computer Science. Like many quantitative majors, social and communications skills may be a concern.

Education Majors - Evaluation of education majors is extremely difficult because of the wide variation in quality between universities. Nationally, GRE test rankings by academic major show that education majors consistently rank in the lowest 25% of knowledge. Any applicant with an education major should be carefully screened for technical skills, and the college ranking checked in US News & World Report's "America's Best Colleges".

International Degrees

A huge variation in quality exists among international degrees. Therefore, J2EE candidates with international degrees should be carefully checked in the "Gourman Report" of International Colleges and Universities.

Some sub-standard overseas colleges have no entrance requirements and require little effort from the student. There has also been a rash of résumé falsifications of college degrees from overseas colleges. The fraudulent applicant is often relying upon the human resource department's inability to successfully contact the overseas school to verify the applicant's degree.

In sum, international degrees should be carefully evaluated. It is recommended that, where appropriate, foreign language professionals are hired to write the letters to request verification of the graduate's attendance, and to obtain and translate the college transcript.

Advanced Degrees and J2EE Professionals

The percentage of J2EE professionals for large corporations possessing an advanced degree (Masters or Doctorate) is increasing. While an advanced degree shows dedication to a professional position, the quality of the degree is of paramount concern.

A higher ranking should be given to an on-site master's degree from a respected university than to a night school or "non-traditional" graduate school. These non-traditional schools often have far lower acceptance standards for students and are far less academically demanding than the top US graduate programs.

The New Graduate

Regardless of the educational experience of the graduate, there will likely be little in his/her background that will prepare him/her for the real-world business environment. Computer curricula tend to emphasize theoretical issues of interest to academicians that may have little direct bearing on the needs of your shop.

The recent graduate may have grandiose visions of designing and maintaining whole software systems. They may be very adept at writing code from scratch, but the fresh graduate will rarely be called upon to do this.

New College graduates are sometimes immature.

Instead, your company will need someone who can work within the existing software system without crashing and burning the edifice down. The paramount skill here is the ability to read OPC (Other People's Code). The candidate with the ability to slog through and understand existing code is the candidate who will be able to add value and make changes in your production system without bringing operations to a grinding halt.

Moreover, the work that the new employee does on the software system will doubtless be modified and altered by others in the future, as new needs develop and hidden problem areas emerge. For this reason, a candidate who is able to show the technical interviewer that he has excellent documentation skills and habits can be a tremendous asset to the company over someone who is not accustomed to submitting work that must be accessible to others. Several of the questions in Chapter 5 are useful for gauging these traits.

Personality of the J2EE Professional

What is more important to managers, technical knowledge or personality? Many times, managers concentrate too much on technical skill, and a candidate's personality is overlooked.

In almost every core job function mentioned above, the J2EE professional's work is made up of interacting with vendors, users, DBAs, managers and even other developers. With that in mind, these professional personality traits are, or ought to be, embodied by the successful Java professional.

Some J2EE programmers have split personalities.

These traits are important for people in almost any profession, but they are particularly important for the J2EE professional. Let it be said of the successful candidate that he or she is self-confident, curious, tenacious, polite, motivated, and a stickler for details.

For some J2EE programmers, everything is an emergency!

Self-confidence

J2EE professionals, especially architects, that lack self-confidence, ask the manager's opinion on every decision no matter how large or small, and show no initiative, are not all-star material. This indecision may be acceptable for an entry level position working under the supervision of a senior J2EE professional, but the candidate should be expected to learn to depend on his or her own judgment for important decisions.

In interviews, questions must be asked about problems encountered and how the applicant would resolve the problems. Answers provided should reflect self-confidence.

A Curious Nature

Curiosity is a core trait of the J2EE professional because the J2EE application platforms, as well as vendor features are constantly changing, and it is sometimes difficult to find examples and document for those changes to the specification or implementation. A J2EE professional who is not curious is passive and reactive, while a curious J2EE professional is proactive. The proactive J2EE professional will install the latest version of a particular J2EE application platform and find enhancements within it that will make their code or design more efficient, easier to read and in many cases make improvements in performance.

Some J2EE programmers don't take initiative.

The curious J2EE professional invests personal money to stay current. In interviews with potential candidates, questions should be asked about the books and subscriptions the candidate relies upon. Needless to say, answers indicating sole reliance on "the documentation set" are not an indication of professional curiosity.

A Tenacious Disposition

Like most disciplines in the IT industry, bulldog-like tenacity is required for troubleshooting as a J2EE developer or architect. The successful candidate should enjoy knuckling down on a problem and not giving up until an answer is found.

In the *comp.lang.java* newsgroup, thousands of questions have been posted by Java and J2EE professionals out in the field. Many times, the questions are about things that would have been solved if the developer had been tenacious and curious instead of giving up.

Polite Manners

A J2EE professional commonly works closely with other people. Therefore, tact is required when dealing with managers, project leads, users, DBAs, and even other developers.

J2EE programmers have a reputation for poor manners!

But here, it should be a fact of life being a J2EE architect or developer. Project managers, DBAs, and users will bring forth unreasonable requests and impossible deadlines. Interpersonal skills must be cultivated by the J2EE professional to respond to such requests without burning bridges. Ill will is fostered outside the application development department by a rude member of the team. The J2EE professional must be extra polite, beginning in the job interview.

Self-Motivating

Employers recognize and value self-starting employees. These are employees who require little in the way of supervision and constant spoon-feeding. Much more in the way of self-motivation is expected from the J2EE professional than other IT professionals; primarily because they are the ones that must take charge of critical architecture and design decisions in order to produce a successful system. In addition, successful J2EE professionals foresee and prevent problems early in the design of a system, and seasoned professionals know what things can cause trouble if they are ignored.

Motivation is a major factor in successful J2EE programming.

A self-motivated J2EE professional will have a history of programming and debugging techniques that can be applied in making the most efficient use of their time during system development.

A self-aware J2EE jockey sees reality clearly.

In an interview, the successful J2EE professional will be able to respond to questions about Java language fundamentals along with complex and distributed application development by talking about the systems they designed and coded. Therefore, the interviewer can craft questions about specific techniques to identify candidates who have actually been involved in critical design and architectural issues within a project.

Detail Orientation

Being detail-oriented is perhaps the most important trait for a J2EE professional. Like most IT professionals, J2EE professionals are often described as having an "anal" personality for their attention to detail, after Sigmund Freud's theory of anal-retentive personalities. A good J2EE candidate should not have to be told to crosscheck details or to document quirks observed during the design or coding phases. A detail-oriented or systematic person is early for an appointment and brings a PDA or calendar to an interview. Questions asked by the detail-oriented person are reflections of the research conducted about the potential new employer.

Attention to Detail is critical for J2EE debugging.

Conclusion

This chapter has been concerned with the specific criteria for evaluating work and academic history. Next, let's look at the roles of a J2EE professional and get more insights into the characteristics of a successful candidate.

A J2EE programmer fluent in Klingon may have a personality disorder.

Roles for the J2EE Professional

Skills assessment

A good J2EE professional candidate will have solid knowledge of techniques in all areas of Java and J2EE. This would include installation, coding and design, packaging, testing and debugging, and use of the Java API libraries. The candidate should also have a firm understanding of all J2EE components and services, knowledge of leading J2EE application frameworks, 3rd party code reuse, and code documentation using Javadoc. In addition, a successful J2EE professional in any organization must possess above average communication skills.

Nit-picky J2EE programmers document everything!

J2EE Professional Job Roles

The job of a J2EE professional means many things to many people. In many cases, the size of the employer will determine what is required from a J2EE professional. In a small shop, their duties are much broader than in corporations with teams of programmers, developers and architects dedicated to specific projects.

The functions of the J2EE professional can also be determined by other factors such as whether the employer is doing custom development. Are they utilizing third party packages that require integration? Will the application be Web based and if so, which J2EE implementation will they be using? The candidate and the interviewer must be prepared to discuss and understand what is expected of the J2EE professional and their role within the company hierarchy.

When a project begins that involves the use of a J2EE application framework, be assured that shortly after the kickoff, many talents within your IT department will be involved including Architects, DBAs, Java programmers, developers and analysts. The J2EE professional will be involved from the start interviewing end users, gathering business requirements, helping set expectations, and mulling over technical design issues. While technical planning and coding remains the most crucial responsibilities of the J2EE professional, many application development shops include other functions within their job function. Here are some common job duties for both J2EE developers and architects:

Produce Specifications – Duties may include working with end users and project managers to write specifications that meet client requirements for applications. The developer/architect will then work with clients and other consultants to plan, develop and code applications according to those specifications.

Gathering and Interpret User Requirements – J2EE professionals should understand how to gather and work with requirements. This often involves Use Cases, UML diagrams, ERD diagrams, and other prototypes. The candidate should understand that the Use Case document is probably the most important in documenting requirements. This document contains the "stories" of how the user will eventually be using the system. It is important that the candidate demonstrates that they have successfully worked with customers in documenting Use Cases and ensuring that they are clearly understood throughout the project life cycle.

Application Testing – Another key function is the ability to work with clients and other team members to test an application's functionality, performance, and load according to specifications. Is the candidate able to demonstrate their success in automating tests, performing unit tests or using a testing framework like JUnit possibly in a complex and distributed application? Can the candidate demonstrate an ability to communicate those results to the proper stakeholders (Team Members, Project Managers, Executive Sponsors, etc.)?

Provide Technical Expertise – The ability to provide technical advice and expertise to other technical team members within a project on system architecture, design and technology alternatives.

Vendor and End-user Liaison - In contacting J2EE software/platform vendor(s) for technical support, the J2EE professional becomes the official company representative and contact point with that vendor and the company. It is often incumbent on the J2EE professional to ensure compliance with the J2EE application platform vendor on license agreements for the company.

To sum up, a full-charge J2EE professional candidate is knowledgeable in installation, project life cycle and methodologies, software configuration management, Java/J2EE security, Java/J2EE application tuning, troubleshooting, vendor relations, and of course, the designing and coding of application systems.

Let's drill-down and review the basic knowledge areas for the J2EE professional candidate.

Purchasing and Installation

The J2EE professional is often involved at the onset in advising, testing and purchasing the J2EE platform software for the company. If this is a requirement, the candidate should be able to work with vendors who implement the J2EE system software to support the application at all levels; operating system, database system, application server, or Web server.

Because each J2EE application framework vendor is different, the successful J2EE candidate should stay current regarding installation and updates on the particular J2EE software platform against which a system is running. Staying current isn't easy. A J2EE professional accustomed to working under Windows NT may have trouble with a UNIX installation. Incorrect updates and invalid configurations performed on production machines can result in big trouble.

In interviews for a J2EE position, questions about installing and upgrading the J2EE application software components systems are to be expected. The candidate should be prepared to discuss his or her platform and any modifications to the standard installation that exist upon it.

Project and Development Life Cycle Methodologies

J2EE candidates should have a basic understanding of project and development life cycle methodologies. Ensure that the J2EE candidate can speak about those projects, which he or she may have worked on that involved providing levels of detail to the project manager using some of the more common life cycle models: spiral model, waterfall model, evolutionary prototyping model, reusable software model, and thruways prototyping model.

Software Configuration Management

J2EE candidates should have a clean understanding of Software Configuration Management tools and concepts. Is the J2EE candidate familiar with the notion of checkout/checkin, branching, merging, version selection rules, work areas, and scopes of visibility?

Application Packaging

Does the candidate have a clear knowledge of how J2EE applications are packaged for deployment? Can they articulate the different file extensions used for EJBs, client applications, and Web modules?

Tool Provider

When designing large and complex distributed applications, it is necessary to advise, recommend, and build tools used to develop, assemble, and package the application. In most cases, the J2EE professional should be familiar with evaluating and recommending what tools should be required by component providers, developers, assemblers, and deployer's.

Application Component Developers

The J2EE professional should demonstrate strong proficiency in his or her ability to develope web components, enterprise beans, application clients, and applets. Questions that can be used to evaluate the J2EE professional in this area are provided in Chapter 5, "The On-site Interview".

Application Assembly

The application assembler is someone responsible for receiving the application component JAR files from the component providers and assembling it into a J2EE application (EAR) file. They will also be responsible for editing and reviewing the deployment descriptors either directly or with tools that add the required XML tags according to the interactive selections within the tool.

This may be the J2EE developer and/or architect performing this role or it may be someone working on the team. Nonetheless, the J2EE professional should know and understand this process and how it will be implemented for the project.

Application Deployer / Administrator

The J2EE professional should have a solid understanding of how J2EE applications are deployed. As a J2EE architect, it is paramount that they understand not only the responsibilities of deploying applications, but also understand how to administer the computing and networking infrastructure where the J2EE applications run in order to oversee the runtime environment.

Does the J2EE candidate provide sufficient evidence of their experiences in developing documentation for the deployment process including setting transaction controls, security attributes, and connections to databases?

Java Security

Having a clear understanding of the J2EE security model is a fundamental skill set in building distributed enterprise applications. Specifically, an understanding of how authentication mechanisms work within the client, EJB, or web tier. Does the candidate know the differences between authentication, authorization, and auditing? What are some of the authorization mechanisms provided by the J2SE and J2EE framework? Also, what mechanisms did the candidate use in the past for controlling access to J2EE resources? Knowledge of how security managers work in Java as well as a clear understating of J2EE services like the "Java Authentication and Authorization Service" (JAAS) is vital to the success in establishing effective security policies within an application.

J2EE/Java Application Tuning

Yet, another one of the skill sets that is often more art than science is application tuning. Given the distributed multi-tiered approach to developing J2EE applications makes the job of tuning even more difficult. It is almost always a requirement that an application not only be designed to solve a particular business problem but be able to perform given a certain set of metrics. This often involves negotiating with end users and setting up user agreements, benchmarking requirements, and sophisticated unit testing.

A successful J2EE developer or architect candidate should be able to bring forward and demonstrate tuning strategies they have used in the past that may or may not have worked. Were they ever called upon to investigate and resolve performance tuning issues at different tiers of an application (i.e. the different J2EE component levels, database, network, host operating system)?

Candidates should be prepared to discuss the pros and cons of Just-In-Time compilers, profiling tools, garbage collection, efficient use of looping, data structures and algorithms, multithreading, and synchronization. They should also be able to discuss their experiences and techniques in tuning complex J2EE applications using load balancing, thread pools, multi-threading techniques, and synchronization.

Troubleshooting

The flair for troubleshooting is a characteristic that is not common to all people. The art of troubleshooting requires an analytical and systematic approach, where the problem is laid out in discrete parts, and each is attacked in a methodical fashion until the problem can be resolved.

A good J2EE programmer is always available!

Troubleshooting sometimes requires the J2EE professional to admit he or she does not know something, but the professional must then have the wherewithal to look for the answer. In responding to questions about troubleshooting, the J2EE candidate should be prepared to discuss real-life experiences. The best examples are those illustrating a lot of thought and multiple troubleshooting steps.

Has the candidate dealt with complex applications that are largely distributed? What techniques did the candidate talk about in troubleshooting the different components of a J2EE application? Did the candidate deal with difficult troubleshooting exercises that dealt with multi-threaded applications, race conditions, and deadlocks?

Communication Skills

Great technical skills are a must for any J2EE professional, but technical knowledge alone does not guarantee job success. As mentioned earlier, a J2EE professional needs to be polite when dealing with team members, managers, vendors, and end users. Because a significant percentage of the J2EE professionals work requires interacting with others on multiple levels, they must be able to speak, think, and write clearly and concisely. A good J2EE professional should strive to set the standard for quality oral and written communication skills.

An inventory of a J2EE professional's communication skills starts with the professional résumé. Their résumé should be easy to read and reflect the candidate's publishing and speaking credits. Whether they were a keynote speaker at a national conference or merely presented a topic at a local user group, those experiences document the candidate's communication skills.

The interviewer should bring questions about job experiences that required the candidate to write documentation or procedures. It should be assumed that candidates with an advanced degree, such as a Masters' or PhD, have well-developed writing skills, or they would not have reached that level of education. Candidates are encouraged to bring to the interview their dissertations or other writing samples.

A successful J2EE professional absolutely must possess strong verbal communication skills. The ability to listen is just as important as the ability to speak clearly. Their daily routine will include listening to complaints and requests, processing that information, and providing responses and instructions.

Conclusion

In sum, the J2EE professional must have a well-rounded skill set, and not just technical skills. An ideal candidate works easily with seasoned professionals as well as being able to manage and engage team members. Add to that excellent communication skills with project leaders and executive management. Next, let's explore screening techniques for J2EE professionals and examine techniques and tools for verifying their technical skill set.

You can always tell a successful J2EE programmer.

Initial Screening

Preparation

Significant amounts of money and other resources can be saved by being thoroughly prepared and paying attention to detail during the screening process. Being prepared can also prevent potentially disastrous problems from ever occurring. Filling vacant positions is expensive, and a careful approach during the initial screening can reap tremendous dividends in the long run.

Be sure to screen for mental health issues!

In the opinion of many IT managers, an effective J2EE professional should have plenty of significant real-world experience to supplement technical knowledge. It has become trendy in the past few years to create sub-categories of J2EE job roles, such as J2EE Developer and J2EE Architect. However, in many large corporations, the J2EE professional is the respected technical guru who participates in all phases of system development, from the initial system analysis to the final physical implementation. Hence, the J2EE professional generally has significant experience in development and systems analysis.

Troubleshooting skills are essential for the J2EE professional

The High Cost of Attrition and Hiring Overhead

The IT industry suffers from one of the highest attrition rates of all professional job categories. This is due, in part, to the dynamic nature of technology, where a job candidate may find himself grossly underpaid and decide to market his skills within a relatively short period of time. The high attrition rate is also due to the lack of challenge within many IT shops that can occur after the job candidate has been successful in their work.

For example, an IT job candidate might enter a shop that needs a great deal of work, only to stabilize the environment to the point where they tend to be bored most of the time. The IT manager must try to distinguish between the "job hopper" and the individual who is changing jobs solely because of a personal need for more challenging work.

The cost of hiring varies by position and by geographic location, but is rarely less than $10,000 per employee. Filling higher end positions, such as Senior J2EE Enterprise Architect can often exceed $50,000, as specialized headhunters are required in order to locate the candidate, and these headhunters commonly charge up to 50 percent of the candidate's first year's wages for a successful placement. There are also the fixed costs of performing background checks and credit checks, as well as HR overhead incurred in checking the individual's transcripts and other resume information.

Choosing Viable Candidates

While reviewing hundreds of applications for a single job, the IT manager must quickly weed-out "posers" and job candidates who do not know their own limitations. To be efficient, the IT manager must quickly drill-down and identify the best three or four candidates to invite for an in-depth technical interview by an experienced J2EE professional. Shops that do not have a current J2EE professional generally hire a J2EE consultant for this task.

J2EE development consultants are commonly asked to help companies find the best J2EE professionals for a permanent position. Later on, we show some of the questions used when evaluating J2EE professional candidates for corporate clients.

"Yes, I know Java, J2EE and two other computer words."

Dealing with IT Headhunters

When seeking a top-level IT position such as Senior J2EE Developer or J2EE Enterprise Architect, it is not uncommon to employ IT headhunters. These IT headhunters can charge up to 50 percent of the IT job's base salary in return for a successful placement.

However, the aggressive nature of the IT headhunters often does a disservice to the IT candidate, and puts the IT manager in a tenuous position. For example, it is not uncommon for the IT manager to receive resumes from two different sources for the same candidate, each represented by different head hunting firms. In cases like this, it is prudent to immediately remove that candidate from the prospective pool, in order to avoid the inevitable feuding between the competing headhunter firms.

When dealing with headhunters, it's also important to get a guarantee that the IT employee will remain in the shop for a period of at least one year and to amortize the payments to the headhunter over that period. Those IT managers who fail to do this may find themselves spending up to $50,000 for a job candidate who quits within ninety days because they are not satisfied with their new job.

It is also important to remember to negotiate the rate with the headhunters. While they may typically command anywhere between 20 and 50 percent of the IT employee's first year gross wages, these terms can indeed be negotiated prior to extending an offer to the IT candidate. In many cases, this works to the disadvantage of the IT candidate, especially when the headhunter refuses to negotiate the terms, thereby making another candidate more financially suitable for the position.

General Evaluation Criteria

Remember, all J2EE professionals are not created equal. They range from the entry-level web programmer to a fully skilled, fire-breathing J2EE Enterprise Architect with extensive credentials.

What level of J2EE professional does the company require? Consider what happens if a fire-breathing J2EE professional is employed in a position that requires only code maintenance of several legacy systems. That fire-breather will soon grow bored and find fertile application development projects elsewhere. On the other hand, hiring an entry-level J2EE web developer for a slot that requires tenacity, drive, initiative, and top-shelf troubleshooting skills is begging for disappointment.

Not all Java programmers have equal intelligence.

It is not easy to match the right candidate for a given position. Given the choice between someone who could write a J2EE EJB container from scratch (but lacks certain personality skills) and a technically inexperienced J2EE web developer who demonstrates the personality traits mentioned above, the less experienced candidate is often the best choice.

The typical entry-level J2EE developer usually has a good-looking résumé that is full of projects and jobs involving Java and

J2EE. However, the interviewer must subtract points if that work involved third-party Integrated Development Environments (IDEs) that were pre-installed and the programmer's main duties were simple code maintenance. When the candidate can't answer in-depth questions concerning the fundamentals of the Java language, deployment descriptors, and developing J2EE components, that person may be a Java-newbie rather than a seasoned J2EE candidate.

Networking skills may be desirable for a Java programmer.

High scores should be given to candidates who have in-depth knowledge of application troubleshooting and unit testing, utilities like Javadoc, policytool, and jdb. Extra points should be given to candidates who have knowledge of J2EE APIs and services like:

- Java Database Connectivity (JDBC)

- Java Naming and Directory Interface (JNDI)

- Java Transaction API (JTA)

- Java Messaging Service (JMS)

- JavaMail

- Java Authentication and Authorization Service (JAAS)

A rule of thumb for hiring J2EE professionals is to avoid hiring an overqualified person who won't be happy in a job with minimal responsibilities. In a shop that utilizes a third-party integrated development environment (IDE) and relies on pre-configured code generators, an entry-level J2EE developer should be hired who can jump into gear whenever required to perform code maintenance.

On the other hand, if a full-charge J2EE professional is needed, a newbie J2EE developer should not be hired, unless the newbie clearly demonstrates the motivation for high-end learning and the desire to become a full-fledged J2EE professional.

Gleaning Demographics from the Candidate

With the advent of strict privacy laws in the United States, the IT manager must be careful never to ask any questions that are inappropriate or illegal. For example, asking the marital status, the number and age of the children, or the age of the applicant himself may make the IT manager vulnerable to age and sex discrimination lawsuits. Hence, the savvy IT manager learns to ask "safe" questions that still reveal the information, while protecting the manager and company from lawsuits.

Do not wind-up in court over an inappropriate interview question!

While the IT manager certainly does not want to discriminate against the job applicant, the demographical aspects of the job applicant nevertheless factor strongly into the hiring decision. For example, the female job applicant who has three children less than five years of age may not be appropriate for an IT position that requires long hours on evenings and weekends.

Another example is age. If the IT manager works for a company that guarantees retirement where age plus years of service equals 70, then hiring a 60-year-old candidate would expose the company to paying that candidate a lifetime pension for only a few years of service.

Elderly Java programmers can add spice to the workplace!

Other important demographical information in our highly mobile society is the depth of connection the IT candidate has to the community. Those IT candidates who do not have extended family, close relatives, and long-term relationships in the community may be tempted to leave the position in order to seek more lucrative opportunities in other geographical areas.

Given that this information is critical to the hiring decision and at the same time inappropriate to ask directly, the savvy IT manager may ask somewhat ambiguous questions in order to get this information. For example, the manager may ask, "What do you do to relax"? This open-ended question will often prompt the candidate to talk about activities they engage in with their families and with the community.

Generally, the selection of a J2EE professional can be accomplished through the following phases:

- Initial screening of résumés by HR department (keyword scan)

- Non-technical screening by IT manager (telephone interview)

- In-depth technical assessment by a senior J2EE professional

- On-site interview (check demeanor, personality, and attitude)

- Background check (verify employment, education, certification)

- Written job offer

Résumé Evaluation

As mentioned, it is not uncommon to receive hundreds of résumés for a particular job position. The goal of the IT manager (or HR department) is to filter through this mountain of résumés and identify the most-qualified candidates for the job interview.

The HR department typically performs a quick filtering through a large stack of resumes in order to narrow the candidates down to a select few, which are in turn presented to the IT manager.

Some resumes may contain anomalies that can reduce the time required for screening. These resume anomalies are known as "red flags", and indicate that the job candidate might not be appropriate for the IT position. These indicators can quickly weed out dozens of candidates, eliminating the need for a more detailed analysis of the resume, saving company resources.

Resume Red Flags

There are several important things to look at when scanning a stack of resumes. The following are a short list that is used by many IT managers:

Unconventional resume formatting and font - Occasionally you may see a nice resume that is done in a professional font, with elaborate graphics, sometimes even including photographs and illustrations. In extreme cases, resumes have been known to arrive printed on pink paper scented with expensive perfumes.

Too much information in the resume - Another red flag for the IT professional is a resume that tends to specify a great deal of non-technical information. For example, the job candidate may go into great detail about their love of certain sports, hobbies, or religious and social activities. In many cases, these resumes indicate an individual for whom the IT profession is not a great priority.

Puffing insignificant achievements - It is not uncommon for low end IT positions to attract job candidates who will exaggerate the importance of trivial training. For example, an IT job candidate may proudly list on his resume that he attended classes on how to use Windows e-mail in the work environment. Of course, trivia within an otherwise nice resume too often indicates a lack of real technical skill, and the job candidate may be making an effort to obfuscate that fact by simply listing anything that they can think of.

Gaps in employment time – It's important to understand that the technically competent IT professional is always in demand and rarely has any kind of gaps in their employment history. Sometimes, IT professionals misrepresent their work chronology in their resumes. For example, if they are laid off and are job seeking for 90 days, they may not list that ninety-day gap of unemployment in order to make themselves seem more attractive. Of course, the start and end dates of each term of employment must be carefully checked by the HR department, and any false indication of this should be grounds for immediate removal from the candidate pool.

Poor grammar and sentence structure - Because the IT industry tends to focus more on technical than verbal skills, you may often find candidates with exceptional technical skills but whose poor writing ability is clearly apparent on their resumes. Short, choppy sentences, incorrect use of verbs, and misspellings can often give you a very good idea of the candidate's ability to communicate effectively via e-mail. Remember, the resume is a carefully crafted and reviewed document. If you find errors in this, you're likely to hire a candidate who lacks adequate written communicative skills.

Short employment periods - Within the IT industry, it is very rare to be dismissed from a position in less than six months. Even the incompetent IT worker is generally given 90 days before they're put on probation and another 90 days before they are dismissed from the job. Hence, an immediate red flag would be any IT employee whose resume indicates that they've worked with an employer for less than 6 elapsed months.

"Yes, I was an NCAA Basketball All-star"
Some job candidate may lie!

Evaluating Training

Scanning résumés involves two factors: evaluation of work history and academic qualifications. Here are some criteria that have been used by major corporations for résumé screening.

J2EE job candidates used to have only two sources for determining their knowledge: experience and/or J2EE training classes. Experience speaks for itself and can be judged as to depth and level of experience. However, any training is only as good as what the candidate puts into the training. In other words, the candidate could either gain much or comparatively little from the experience of training, depending on whether they took their "will to learn" and curiosity with them to class.

As I have noted, Java and J2EE certification (offered by Sun Microsystems) is one benchmark of a modicum of competence. The exams test the candidate's knowledge in all areas of the professional skill set from Java language fundamentals to architecting enterprise J2EE applications.

In order to pass, a candidate, in almost all cases, will need to have had actual experience as a Java/J2EE developer and will need to have knowledge from multiple references. These tests were developed by over a dozen highly skilled and experienced J2EE professionals and have been certified against hundreds of J2EE candidates. While obtaining a J2EE certification from these exams is no absolute guarantee that a candidate is fully qualified, it can be used as an acid test to separate the wheat from the chaff.

"I've been programming in Java for 35 years."

Telephone Screening

After reviewing the available resumes, you will be in a position to select from a pool of candidates for further telephone screening. The telephone interview is a useful tool for weeding those candidates whose actual qualities may not quite match their glowing resumes, saving considerable time and expense over on-site interviews.

The interview may be either unscheduled or prearranged. In both cases, the candidate will be less prepared than for the more formal on-site interview, and it can quickly become apparent that a candidate is inappropriate to fill the position.

The telephone is your best tool for pre-screening technical skills.

The unscheduled telephone screening is an opportunity to discover how well the candidate thinks on his feet and provides insight into his unrehearsed thoughts and feelings. It can also indicate how well the candidate is organized, since the person who has to repeatedly search for basic necessary materials and documents at home is unlikely to demonstrate superior efficiency in the work environment.

The interviewer should cover all pertinent areas, with the goal of confirming the qualifications present in the resume. The candidate should be well informed about those topics which the resume indicates are areas of proficiency.

The telephone interview will also reveal a great deal about non-technical qualifications. Is the candidate personable and articulate? How well do they listen?

The information and impressions gathered from the telephone screening will enable the IT manager to confidently select the best-qualified candidates for an in-depth technical interview.

Technical Pre-Testing

The job interview questions in this text are deliberately intended to be presented orally. While these questions often indicate a high degree of experience and skill with a specific technology, many IT managers will require the job candidate to take an in-depth technical examination.

The technical examination may be given over the Internet, using job-testing sites such as Brain Bench, or they may be paper and pencil tests administered to the candidate before the start of a detailed job interview.

There are important legal ramifications for the use of these testing methods. Many job candidates who are not selected for an important position may challenge both the scope and validity of the test itself. These challenges have been applied even to nationally known aptitude tests such as the SAT and LSAT exams; IT exams and language tests such as C++, C#, and you guessed it – Java and J2EE. These tests may be especially prone to challenge by the disgruntled IT professional.

While it is important to do a complete check of all the technical abilities of the IT candidate, it is very important for the IT manager never to cite the failure of one of these exams as the reason for removal from the applicant pool. This is a common technique used by IT managers when they find a particular candidate's knowledge of the field to be insufficient.

For example, in a highly competitive IT vacancy, very small things may wind up making the difference. In any case, when rejecting a candidate, the IT manager should generally cite something intangible, such as the job skills do not completely meet the requirements of the position, or a more nebulous answer, such as the candidate's interpersonal skills will not mesh with the team environment. Remember, specific citation of failure of any tangible IT testing metric may open your company to challenges and lawsuits.

Developing Questions for Interviews

Interview questions should be diligently researched and the expected answers listed prior to the interview. Where open-ended questions are used, the interviewer should have the level of knowledge required to judge the correctness of the answers given by the candidate.

You cannot always identify drug users

The questions should be broken into categories and each should be assigned a point value based on either a scale, such as from 0-5 or according to difficulty. Technically competent personnel should review interview questions for accuracy and applicability.

At the conclusion of the interview, evaluation of technical ability should be based on the results from these points. In addition, "open-ended" questions should be included, such as "Describe the most challenging problem you have solved to date", or "Name one item that you have developed that you are most proud of (in software development)". These open-ended questions are designed to allow the J2EE job candidate to articulate and demonstrate their communications skills.

The IT Candidate's Demeanor

During the face-to-face interview, the IT manager can glean a great deal about the personality of the individual simply by observing his/her body language and listening to the candidate speak. In many cases, the IT manager may base the assessment of the interview candidate on non-technical criteria; especially the behavior of the candidate when asked pointed questions. Some of these demeanor factors include:

Eye Contact

IT candidates who are unwilling or unable to maintain eye contact with the interviewer may not possess the interpersonal skills required to effectively communicate with end-users and co-workers.

Fidgeting

IT candidates who are experiencing high anxiety during an interview may cross and uncross their legs, sit uncomfortably, or twiddle their hair while speaking with the IT manager. These involuntary signs of discomfort may indicate that the candidate does not function well in the stressful environment of a busy IT shop.

Diction

For those IT positions that require exceptional communicative skills, such as working with the end-user community, you can get a very good idea of the abilities of the job candidates simply by listening to their responses. For example, careful IT professionals may demonstrate the "lawyer's pause" before answering the question. This pause, of about two seconds, often indicates that the job candidate is thinking carefully and formulating his response before speaking.

Job candidates who formulate their answers carefully can be especially useful in those positions where the risk of damage from impulsive verbal statements, without considering the consequences of the statement, is high. You can also assess how articulate the job candidate is by the use of filler words such as "you know", inappropriate pauses, poor diction structure, poor choice of words, and a limited vocabulary.

"My long-term career goal?
Actually, I want to get your job."

Appropriate Appearance

A professional job candidate who doesn't take the time to put the best foot forward by maintaining proper appearance probably doesn't have the wherewithal to perform adequately in the job. Clean, appropriate clothing and proper grooming show that the candidate is willing to make the effort to please the employer. Candidates who are sloppy in appearance and mannerisms will bring those characteristics to the job and to their interactions with other parts of the company.

Make sure your Java programmer understands proper dress codes.

Savvy candidates will adopt the dress of the executive and banking industry. This attire generally includes:

- Crisp white shirt
- Conservative tie

- Dark suit
- Dark leather shoes

Proper job interview attire is important.

We will take a closer look at the on-site interview in the next chapter.

Conducting the Background Check

As we have repeatedly noted, a candidate's references must always be rigorously checked. Previous employers should be spoken with, if possible, to learn about a candidate's past work history. Many people are good at interviewing but won't necessarily function in the job.

Because of the explosive growth of the IT industry, fraudulent resumes have become increasingly common. Job candidates have been known to fabricate their college educations and the scope of their work experience, smooth over gaps in their employment history, and exaggerate their job skills. In some cases, job skills may be exaggerated inadvertently, because the job candidate has only a brief exposure to a technology and does not understand their own limitations.

Therefore, it is very important for the HR department to perform a complete resume check before forwarding any of these candidates for detailed interviews by the IT manager. These background checks may require the candidate's waiver signature for the release of all medical, criminal, and credit-related records.

The high rate of fraud found in resume applications has spawned a new industry of private investigators, who for a fixed fee, will check national databases, revealing any criminal activity on the part of the job candidate, a history of bad credit, and other moral and demographic factors that may be relevant to their suitability for the position.

Making the Initial Job Offer

Once the IT manager has chosen the right candidate, it is common to make an offer based on nation-wide studies of the average salaries within the geographical area. For example, IT application shops in expensive, professional urban areas, such as New York City, will earn twice as much as an IT professional with the same skills, working in a cheaper suburban or rural area.

If you decide to make an offer to a candidate, it is a good idea to ask them the salary amount they have in mind. If the candidate is the first to mention a number, the company is placed in an advantageous negotiating position.

If the candidate indicates he will be satisfied with an amount that is lower than you were prepared to offer, then you have arrived at the ideal hiring scenario. You have a candidate that you have already decided is desirable for the position, and they will take less money than you had anticipated paying them.

On the other hand, if the candidate has an unreasonably high expectation given his skill level and the market in your area, he may have an unrealistic view of the current business environment. This can indicate either that the candidate didn't do his homework or simply wishful thinking. You might point out that the range for this position is somewhat lower than he anticipates. You can then offer the amount you originally had in mind, and negotiate from there.

The savvy IT manager will try to offer a candidate with an excellent set of IT skills a balance between the "going rate" and other intangible benefits, in order to make the job appealing. Other intangibles might include additional vacation time, flextime, telecommuting, and other perks designed to make the job more attractive to the candidates.

Of course, the IT manager may deliberately reduce the size of the initial offer if he anticipates that the candidate may negotiate for more. A highly desirable IT candidate may be courted by multiple companies and will often respond to the job offer with a counteroffer, citing other employers who are willing to pay more for the same skill set. When this happens, the IT manager may soon be faced with the dilemma of paying more than they desired for the candidate, and may also question the candidate's motive in earning a high salary.

Conclusion

In sum, while the recession of 2002 created a shakeout within the lower ranks of J2EE professionals, IT managers remain committed to retaining their top Java and J2EE talent, and those J2EE professionals with specialized skills are still in high demand.

In today's highly volatile work environment, the average Java professional rarely stays with a single employer for a long period of time. Competition remains extremely strong for those Java and J2EE superstars whose skill and background make them indispensable. While some attrition of J2EE professionals is inevitable, there are many techniques that savvy IT managers can use to retain their top talent.

At this point, you should be ready to invite the candidate for an on-site interview. Let's look at an approach to conducting a technical interview to access the candidate's level of technical J2EE knowledge.

The On-site Interview

CHAPTER 5

Evaluation

During the on-site interview, the J2EE professional needs to be evaluated for both technical skills and non-technical personality traits that will indicate whether the candidate can be successful in your work environment.

Now it's your turn to ask the tough questions!

The specific areas that you choose to emphasize in the interview will depend on the nature of the position. A System's Architect who coordinates the efforts of several people will need a different skill set than someone who primarily works only on code maintenance. Choose questions that will highlight the specific skills you need and look for past experiences that demonstrate those abilities.

An effective J2EE professional must be able to wear many hats. He must have the necessary discipline in managing multiple and in many times conflicting tasks, the interpersonal skills involved in communicating with team members and project managers, and of most importance, the technical skills in Java, J2EE components, and J2EE services. This may include but is not limited to Object Oriented programming techniques, accessing relational databases using JDBC, writing web components (Servlets and JSPs), coding and designing Enterprise Java Beans, and many other Java and J2EE language fundamentals. Ask questions that demonstrate these abilities and look for experiences that show accomplishments in these areas.

Questions from the Candidate

Most books and articles neglect to discuss the questions that the candidate may ask the interviewer. This is unfortunate, because whether or not the candidate asks questions, and the character of those questions, can reveal a lot about his personality and suitability for the job.

After all, the serious candidate is evaluating the company just as you are evaluating him. If he is able to ask intelligent questions that are intended to assess how well his particular abilities and goals will integrate with the job, he is actually doing part of your job for you.

A certain amount of nervousness is inherent to the interview process, but the passive candidate who appears reluctant or unable to answer interview questions, as if under cross-examination, can only raise suspicions about the reason for his reticence. Contrast this person with the engaging candidate who doesn't answer so much as he conversationally responds, volunteering the pertinent information while interspersing his responses with questions of his own.

The candidate's questions should focus on the tasks and responsibilities he will encounter in the performance of his job. If the candidate takes the initiative in this way, facilitating the interview as you mutually explore whether the position is a good fit, chances are he will bring this same constructive approach to the work environment once you determine that he is, indeed, the best person for the job.

Beware the candidate who only seems to be interested in his salary and the other perks that he will enjoy. There will be time to discuss money once you both decide that the alliance between you is promising. The thrust of the interview should be on the requirements of the position and whether the candidate is equipped to meet them.

Telephone Pre-interview Questions

At some point in the process, you will be faced with a number of high quality resumes in your file. Committing to an on-site interview costs time and money for both parties. It is therefore important to consider some pre-interview checking. Performing a telephone interview to pre-screen geographically remote candidates can help in avoiding travel costs associated with an on-site interview. Also, ask to see their previous work or contact a former employer. As long as you remain discrete this is generally not going to be an issue.

The following 10 questions should help in determining the technical skill set of any potential J2EE candidate. The questions are simple enough that any qualified J2EE professional should me able to answer them immediately from memory. If a candidate has a hard time with these questions, they may not be appropriate for a full time position as a J2EE Developer or Architect.

1. When working with a *Web application*, what is the filename of the deployment descriptor and where should be it located?

   The name of the deployment descriptor for web applications is named web.xml and is typically located in the (web-app-root)/WEB-INF/web.xml.

2. What is the name of the XML root element within the Web deployment descriptor file; web.xml?

   The name of the XML root element is <web-app>.

3. What are the two J2EE Web-based technologies that support dynamic content generation of web pages in a portable and cross-platform manner?

   JavaServer Pages (JSP) and Servlets.

4. You have a client application that needs to lookup the home interface of an enterprise bean. Which class and method is used to lookup the bean?

   The application would need to use the lookup() method of the InitialContext class, found in the JNDI package. In order to access an enterprise bean, the application will use the JNDI package to obtain a directory connection to a beans container. Once the connection is established, a new InitialContext object is created. The lookup() method of the InitialContext object is then used to look up the bean.

The lookup() method will return a reference to the home object of the bean.

5. What are the two ways in which an *entity bean* can persist enterprise data?

An entity can use either container-managed persistence (CMP) or bean-managed persistence. With CMP, the EJB container is responsible for handling the implementation of code (SQL) necessary to insert, read, and update an object in a data source. With BMP, the application developer needs to create the implementation code for the insert, read, and update of an object.

6. You have an application that uses Java objects exclusively. Which distributed technology should you consider for communication; RMI or CORBA? Why?

If you have an application that only contains Java objects, it would be appropriate to use RMI. The RMI technology is built right into the Java language as a means of allowing objects to communicate with other objects that are running on JVMs on remote machine within the network. Using CORBA technology, objects that are exported with CORBA can be accessed by clients implemented in any language (C, Perl, etc) with an IDL binding. Although CORBA is more extensive than RMI, RMI is more straightforward to use since it only used Java objects.

7. You are about the write a *Session Bean*. What are the three types of component (classes and interfaces) that are needed to write a Session Bean?

To write a session bean, you will need to create the following:

- Home Interface

- Remote Interface
- The actual bean class which implements the SessionBean Interface

8. Suppose you have an HTTP servlet that overrides the doGet() method for receiving GET requests. What are the names of the two classes passed into the doGet() method that will allow you to receive requests and to respond to the web client?

> The two object types are HttpServletRequest and HttpServletResponse. The HttpServletRequest object represents the client's request and provides the servlet with access to information about the client, the parameters for the request, and the HTTP headers passed along with the request. The HttpServletResponse object represents the servlet's response and is used to return data to the client.

> Here is the signature of an example doGet() method:

```
public void doGet(
  HttpServletRequest req
, HttpServletResponse res
)
throws ServletException, IOException {}
```

9. Given an HTTP PUT method, what is the corresponding method in the HttpServlet class that will be called upon invocation?

> The doPut() method. The doPut() method of the HttpServlet abstract class is used to handle the HTTP PUT type request.

10. In a Java Server Page (JSP), how would you declare a String object named firstName and assign it the value of "*Alex*"?

> <%! String firstName = new String("Alex"); %>

Technical Questions

The following questions were developed in case noone in your organization is qualified to assess the job candidate's skill set. Even without detailed knowledge of Java and J2EE, you can get a vague idea of the technical skills of your J2EE professional job candidate.

While this quick technical check can be administered over the telephone, it is often performed on-site by a Sun Certified J2EE Professional. Each question attempts to be unambiguous with a clear and accurate answer.

The interviewer should begin by apologizing for asking pointed technical questions before reading each question verbatim. If a candidate asks for clarification or says that he or she does not understand the question, the interviewer re-reads the question. If the candidate fails to answer a question or answers incorrectly, the interviewer should respond "OK," and move immediately to the next question.

IMPORTANT NOTE:

The intention of this section is not to provide a comprehensive J2EE technical exam – the technical questions are only intended to be examples. The only way to accurately evaluate the skills of a J2EE job applicant is to employ the services of an experienced J2EE developer and conduct an in-depth technical interview and skills assessment. An experienced J2EE developer should administer the interview questions presented in this book.

Java and J2EE Versions

Several of the expected answers from these questions may be highly dependent upon the version of Java and the J2EE specification. While I have made every effort to make the questions as version neutral as possible, each release of the J2EE specification brings many changes and new features, and these example questions may not be appropriate for your version of Java/J2EE implementation. As a reference when determining whether behavior and syntax is correct, I use Sun's J2EE 1.3 platform specification.

Qualifications

1. Do you have any Certifications? (i.e. Java Programmer/Developer, Cisco, Microsoft, Oracle)

    Answer: _____

    Comment: _____

2. What relational database systems are you most familiar with? (Oracle, SQL Server, MySQL, Postgres, etc.)

    Answer: _____

    Comment: _____

3. What J2EE Application Servers are you most familiar with? (Oracle9iAS, OC4J, BEA WebLogic Server, IBM WebSphere, JBoss, etc.)

    Answer: _____

    Comment: _____

4. Which Java Development IDE are you most comfortable with? (JBuilder, IntelliJ IDEA, JDeveloper, plain 'ol Emacs, etc.)

Answer: _____

Comment: _____

5. Which version control systems have you used in the past? (CVS, Oracle Software Configuration Management, Continuus, ClearCase, etc.)

Answer: _____

Comment: _____

6. Highest level of education?

Most candidates in this field require a college education, preferably a BS in computer science, computer information technology or related engineering field.

Answer: _____

Comment: _____

J2EE Development Concepts

1. A J2EE application is divided into components based on the function they need to support. What are the components defined in the J2EE specification?

    Skill Level: Low

    Expected answer:

    Application clients and applets are components that run on the client machine.

    Score: _____

    Notes: _____

    _____

2. Java Servlets and JavaServer Pages (JSP) are web-based components that run within a web container on the server.

    Skill Level: Low

    Expected answer:

    Enterprise JavaBeans (EJB) components (also known as enterprise beans) are business components that are run within an EJB container on the server.

    Score: _____

    Notes: _____

    _____

3. What is the Remote Method Invocation (RMI) Protocol?

Skill Level: Intermediate

Expected answer:

Remote Method Invocation (RMI) is a set of APIs that allows developers to build distributed applications using the Java programming language. Defined in the Java language, RMI uses interfaces to define remote objects with a combination of Java serialization and the Java Remote Method Protocol (JRMP) to turn local method invocations into remote method invocation.

Score: _____

Notes: _____

_____

4. What is the Java Remote Method Protocol (JRMP)?

Skill Level: High

Expected answer:

Java Remote Method Protocol (JRMP) is a proprietary wire-level protocol designed by Sun Microsystems to support the transparent mechanism required for communication between objects in the Java language that reside in different address spaces. The J2EE supports the JRMP protocol but does not appear to use the term any longer; simply referring to it as the "RMI transport protocol". JRMP basically serves the same function as IIOP, but also supports object passing.

Score: _____

Notes: _____

_____

5. What is a deployment descriptor?

Skill Level: Low

Expected answer:

A deployment descriptor is an XML file that accompanies each module of a J2EE application. It describes the specific configuration requirements that need to be resolved for the module or application to be installed successfully to an application server.

Score: _____

Notes: _____

_____

6. J2EE Enterprise Applications, with all of their modules (web, client, business tier), are packaged into what type of file?

Skill Level: Low

Expected answer:

They are packaged into an Enterprise Archive (EAR) file. An EAR file is nothing more than a standard Java Archive (JAR) file with an .ear extension.

Score: _____

Notes: _____

_____

7. What types of files and modules can be found in an Enterprise Archive (EAR) file?

Skill Level: Low

Expected answer:

An EAR file can comprise WAR, EJB JAR, RAR, and JAR files along with the application descriptor file; application.xml.

Score: _____

Notes: _____

_____

8. What are Web archive (WAR) files? What is the standard file extension to a WAR file?

Skill Level: Low

Expected answer:

A WAR file is used to package *Web modules* for the purpose of deploying them to an application server. A WAR file has a standard file extension .war. A Web Archive (WAR) file is a Java archive file (created using the jar utility) used to store one or more of the following:

- Descriptive meta-information

- Java Servlets

- JavaServer Pages (JSP)

- Utility libraries and classes

- Static documents, such as HTML files, images, and possibly sound files.

- Client-side programs like applets, beans, and classes.

A Web module can represent a stand-alone Web application, or it can be combined with other modules (for example, EJB modules) to form a full J2EE application.

Score: _____

Notes: _____

_____

9. What are the two transport protocols used by J2EE web-based client applications?

Skill Level: Low

Expected answer:

Web clients can use either the HTTP or HTTPS transport protocol.

Score: _____

Notes: _____

_____

10. What is the Enterprise Information System (EIS) Tier within the J2EE environment?

Skill Level: Intermediate

Expected answer:

The EIS tier includes your backend and legacy systems and normally includes the companies' Enterprise Resource Planning (ERP) system, mainframe transaction processing systems, database systems, and other legacy information systems. A typical J2EE enterprise application will need to communicate request and response processing with these legacy systems within the EIS Tier. Integrating new J2EE application with the EIS tier has assumed great importance because enterprises are striving to leverage their existing systems and resources while adopting and developing new technologies and architectures.

Score: _____

Notes: _____

_____

11. What is the standard architecture used for connecting to the Enterprise Information System (EIS) tier from the J2EE platform?

Skill Level: High

Expected answer:

The J2EE Connector Architecture.

Score: _____

Notes: _____

_____

12. What are some of the types of containers defined in the J2EE architecture and what are they used for? Where are they located (client, application server, database server)?

Skill Level: Low

Expected answer:

Application client container - This type of container is found on the client machine and is responsible for running and managing the execution of all application client components for a single J2EE application. An applet container, for example, is a combination of a web browser and Java plug-in located on the client machine.

EJB container - The EJB container is responsible for running and managing the execution of all enterprise beans for a single J2EE application. The EJB container is run on the application server.

Web container - A web container is responsible for running and managing the execution of all JSP and servlet components for a single J2EE application. The web container and its components are run on the application server.

Score: _____

Notes: _____

_____

13. Why would you use a modeling tool for designing a J2EE application?

Skill Level: Low

Expected answer:

Modeling tools are used to because of the increasing complexity of today's enterprise application systems and their components. These tools allow you to visualize the processes used for constructing and documenting the design and structure of an application. They also provide a means for showing the many components, their interdependencies, and how they relate to other components and subsystems in a large and complex application.

Score: _____

Notes: _____

_____

14. What is the most popular modeling tool used for designing large and complex J2EE applications?

Skill Level: Low

Expected answer:

The Unified Modeling Language (UML).

Score: _____

Notes: _____

_____

15. What is a transaction?

Skill Level: Intermediate

Expected answer:
A transaction is a bracket of processing or a sequence of information exchange and related work that represents a logical unit of work. It can be thought of as an "all or nothing" contract; all of the processing must be completed or else the transaction management component (sometimes called a transaction monitor) should restore (rollback) the application to the status as it was before the start of the transaction.

Score: _____

Notes: _____

_____

16. What is ACID as it relates to transactions?

Skill Level: High

Expected answer:
ACID is an acronym used to describe the four primary attributes ensured to any transaction by a transaction

Conducting the J2EE Job Interview

manager (sometimes called a transaction monitor or TP monitor). These attributes are:

Atomicity. In a transaction involving two or more discrete pieces of information, either all of the pieces are committed or none are. This is sometimes referred to as the "all-or-nothing" property. This property defines that the entire sequence of operations are successful or the entire sequence is entirely unsuccessful. Successfully completed transactions are committed, while unsuccessful (partially executed) transactions are rolled back.

Consistency. Transaction must always work on a consistent view of data. Also, when a transaction ends, it must leave the data in a consistent state. This property ensures that a transaction never leaves the database in a half-finished state. While a transaction is executing, it may be possible for certain constraints be violated (as with deferred transactions), but no other transaction will be allowed to see these inconsistencies. When the transaction ends, all such inconsistencies will have been eliminated.

Isolation. For a given transaction that is in process and not yet committed, it must remain isolated from any other transaction. This property keeps transactions separated from each other until they're finished. For a given transaction, it should appear as though it is running all by itself — the effects of other concurrently running transactions on the system are invisible to this transaction. The effects of this transaction are invisible to others until the transaction is committed.

Durability. This property defines that the results of any committed data is permanent. Committed data is saved by the system such that, even in the event of a failure and system restart, the data is available in its correct state.

Score: _____

Notes: _____

_____

17. Are JAR files meant to be platform independent?

Skill Level: Low

Expected answer:

Yes. JAR files are based on the popular ZIP file format and are cross-platform so developers do not have to worry about platform issues.

Score: _____

Notes: _____

_____

18. What is the protocol used for communicating between CORBA object request brokers (ORBs)?

Skill Level: Intermediate

Expected answer:

Internet Inter-ORB Protocol (IIOP)

Score: _____

Notes: _____

_____

19. What is Remote Method Invocation (RMI)?

   Skill Level: Low

   Expected answer:
   RMI is a distributed object model that allows a Java object running in one Java Virtual Machine (JVM) to invoke methods on another Java object running in a different JVM.

   Score: _____

   Notes: _____

   _____

20. You are designing a J2EE application that needs to implement asynchronous messaging? Which J2EE service would you use?

   Skill Level: Low

   Expected answer:
   Java Message Service (JMS).

Score: _____

Notes: _____

_____

21. Which J2EE service API would you use to allow applications and J2EE servers to use transactions?

Skill Level: Low

Expected answer*:*
Java Transaction API (JTA).

Score: _____

Notes: _____

_____

Java Database Connectivity (JDBC)

1. What is the Java Database Connectivity API?

    Skill Level: Low

    Expected answer:

    > The Java Database Connectivity API (or JDBC for short) provides database access to Java applications in a vendor independent manner. When using the JDBC API, a Java application can perform database access independent of the actual database engine. The same Java application can be written once, compiled once, and run against any database engine with a JDBC driver.

    Score: _____

    Notes: _____

    _____

2. The JDBC API consists of which two packages?

    Skill Level: Intermediate

    Expected answer:

    > java.sql and javax.sql (which provides for server-side capabilities)

    Score: _____

    Notes: _____

    _____

3. What are the different ways to establish a connection to a database using JDBC?

Skill Level: High

Expected answer:

Registering the driver using DriverManager.

```
DriverManager.registerDriver(
  new oracle.jdbc.driver.OracleDriver());

Connection con =
  DriverManager.getConnection(
     "jdbc:oracle:thin:@bartman:1521:O920DB"
  , "scott"
  , "tiger");
```

Setting the "jdbc.drivers" system properties.

```
System.setProperty(
    "jdbc.drivers"
  , "oracle.jdbc.driver.OracleDriver");

Connection con =
  DriverManager.getConnection(
     "jdbc:oracle:thin:@bartman:1521:O920DB"
  , "scott"
  , "tiger");
```

Using the classForName method.

```
Class.forName("oracle.jdbc.driver.OracleDriver").newInsta
nce();

Connection con =
  DriverManager.getConnection(
     "jdbc:oracle:thin:@bartman:1521:O920DB"
  , "scott"
  , "tiger");
```

Score: _____

Notes: _____

_____

4. What does it mean when you get a "No suitable driver" error from your JDBC application? What should you look for when approached with this error?

Skill Level: High

Expected answer:

The error, "No suitable driver" typically occurs during a call to the DriverManager.getConnection method. The usual cause can be failing to load the appropriate JDBC drivers before calling the getConnection method. It may also be that you are specifying an invalid JDBC URL - one that isn't recognized by your JDBC driver.

The first thing to check is the documentation for the JDBC driver you are using.

This problem can also be seen when attempting to use the JDBC-ODBC Bridge and one or more of the shared libraries needed by the Bridge cannot be loaded. If you believe this is the case, check your configuration to be sure that any required shared libraries are accessible to the Bridge.

Score: _____

Notes: _____

_____

5. You have a JDBC connection object named con. How would you turn off *auto-committing* for this connection?

Skill Level: Low

Expected answer:

Use the setAutoCommit method of the Connection class passing in the boolean value false.

```
con.setAutoCommit(false);
```

Score: _____

Notes: _____

_____

6. You have a ResultSet object named rset that you want to retrieve data from. How would you retrieve all of the data from within a while loop?

Skill Level: Intermediate

Expected answer:

```
String query = "SELECT * FROM my_table";
ResultSet rset = stmt.executeQuery(query);
while (rset.next()) {
  // Use the rset.getXXX methods to
  // retrieve data
}
```

7. What are some of the getXXX methods in the ResultSet class used to retrieve values?

Skill Level: Low

Expected answer:

Assuming a ResultSet object named rset, here are some examples:

```
BigDecimal bd = rset.getBigDecimal(1);
Blob       bl = rset.getBlob(2);
boolean    bn = rset.getBoolean(3);
byte       bt = rset.getByte(4);
Clob       cl = rset.getClob(5);
Date       dt = rset.getDate(6);
double     dl = rset.getDouble(7);
float      ft = rset.getFloat(8);
int         i = rset.getInt(9);
long        l = rset.getLong(10);
short       s = rset.getShort(11);
String     st = rset.getString(12);
```

Score: _____

Notes: _____

_____

8. How would you select an entire row of data from a ResultSet in one command instead of calling an individual ResultSet.getXXX method for each column?

Skill Level: High

Expected answer:

As of the JDBC API 3.0 (at the time of this writing), this is not possible. Using the ResultSet.getXXX methods is the only way to retrieve data from a ResultSet object – this means you will need to make the method call for each column of the row being returned.

Score: _____

Notes: _____

_____

9. Is it possible to get a count of the number of columns returned from a ResultSet object? If so, how?

Skill Level: High

Expected answer:

It is possible to get a column count, but not directly from the ResultSet object. It is possible, however, to instantiate a ResultSetMetaData object (from the ResultSet) and use the getColumnCount() method. The following code provides an example:

```
ResultSet rset =
    stmt.executeQuery("select * from test");

ResultSetMetaData rsMeta = rset.getMetaData();

System.out.println(
    "Number of columns: " +
    rsMeta.getColumnCount()
);
```

Score: _____

Notes: _____

_____

10. Is there a method that could be used to return the number of rows returned from a ResultSet? If so, what is the name of the method? If not, what is the easiest way to capture the number of rows returned?

Skill Level: High

Expected answer:

No. There is no direct method you could call, but it is easy to find the number of rows. Let's say you have a scrollable result set, rset, you can call the methods rset.last and then rset.getRow to find out how many rows rset has. If the result set is not scrollable, you can either (1) count the rows by iterating through the result set or (2) get the number of rows by submitting a query with a COUNT column in the SELECT clause.

Score: _____

Notes: _____

_____

11. You have an application using JDBC connection pooling. Which interface is used as the resource manager connection factory for pooled connection objects (java.sql.Connection objects)?

Skill Level: Intermediate

Expected answer:

PooledConnectionDataSource

Score: _____

Notes: _____

_____

Java Servlets

1. What are the two objects passed to the servlet's service method in a servlet that extends the HttpServlet class?

   Skill Level: Low

   Expected answer:

   The two objects passed are HttpServletRequest and HttpServletResponse. The service method then passes the same two parameters to the appropriate doPut, doGet, or doPost, method in the servlet that extends the HttpServlet class.

   Score: _____

   Notes: _____

   _____

2. What is the name of the *deployment descriptor* for a web application and which directory do you place this file relative to the context (document) root directory?

   Skill Level: Low

   Expected answer:

   The name of the web application deployment descriptor is named web.xml and is placed in the /WEB-INF/ directory.

   Score: _____

   Notes: _____

   _____

3. What is the corresponding method in the HttpServlet class for an HTTP POST method call?

Skill Level: Low

Expected answer:
`doPost`

Score: _____

Notes: _____

_____

4. Where should all servlet class files be placed relative to the context (document) root?

Skill Level: Low

Expected answer:
All classes should be placed in the WEB-INF/classes directory.

Score: _____

Notes: _____

_____

5. For a servlet, what method is used to return an Enumeration of String objects that represent the values of all request parameters, as with HTML form parameters?

Skill Level: Intermediate

Expected answer:

You would use the getParameterNames() method of the request object as shown in the following example:

```
Enumeration params =
      req.getParameterNames();
```

Score: _____

Notes: _____

_____

6. Servlet containers support the ability to store startup parameters and make them available to the servlet when it is initiated. How would you retrieve an initialization parameter in a servlet?

Skill Level: Intermediate

Expected answer:

You would use two methods: getServletConfig() and getInitParameter("paramName") to return the value as a string as shown in the following example:

```
String myValue =
   getServletConfig().getInitParameter ("myParamName");
```

Score: _____

Notes: _____

_____

7. How many times does the service method and init method get called for a servlet?

Skill Level: Low

Expected answer:

The service method will be called for every request to the servlet. The init method, on the other hand, is only called one time, and that is when the servlet is being initialized.

Score: _____

Notes: _____

_____

8. What is the purpose of the init method of a servlet and what is the parameter passed to the init method?

Skill Level: Low

Expected answer:

The init method of a servlet is called by the servlet container to indicate to the servlet that it is being placed into service. You can override this method in your servlet to set certain initialization information for your servlet. The init method is passed in a ServletConfig object.

Score: _____

Notes: _____

_____

9. Briefly describe the order in which servlets get loaded defined in the deployment descriptor file?

Skill Level: Intermediate

Expected answer:

The servlet container will first load those servlets that are declared to (have the element) "**load-on-startup**" in the order they are listed in the deployment descriptor. For those servlets that do not have the **load-on-startup** element defined, there is no guarantee when it will be loaded by the servlet container.

Score: _____

Notes: _____

_____

10. What is the name of the method and interface used to redirect an HTTP request to another URL?

Skill Level: Low

Expected answer:

You would use the interface / method as a response to the client to redirect it to a new URL:

```
HttpServletResponse.sendRedirect("newUrl")
```

Here is an example:

```
String newUrl = "../RedirectedPage.html";
response.sendRedirect(newUrl);
```

Score: _____

Notes: _____

_____

11. You need to write a servlet that prints the name/value pairs of all HTTP request header parameters. Suppose that you already have a PrintWriter object named out and a HttpServletRequest object named request in your servlet. Write the code to print all HTTP request header parameters?

Skill Level: High

Expected answer:
```
...
Enumeration head = request.getHeaderNames();
while (head.hasMoreElements()) {
  String headerName = (String) head.nextElement();
  String headerValue = request.getHeader(headerName);
  out.println("NAME = " + headerName);
  out.println("VALUE = " + headerValue);
}
...
```

Score: _____

Notes: _____

_____

12. You have a Web application that contains servlets and several Java JAR libraries that are needed to support the application (i.e. JDBC drivers like ojdbc14.jar). Which directory should the Java JAR libraries be placed relative to the context (document) root?

Skill Level: Low

Expected answer:
All JAR files should go in the /WEB-INF/lib/ directory.

Score: _____

Notes: _____

_____

13. What is the name of the XML element defined in the deployment descriptor file that is used by the container to pass initialization parameters to a servlet?

Skill Level: Intermediate

Expected answer:

<init-param>. Here is an example from a web.xml file:

```
<servlet>
  <servlet-name>PrintInitParameters</servlet-name>
  <servlet-class>PrintInitParameters</servlet-class>
  <init-param>
    <param-name>jdbcClassDriver</param-name>
    <param-value>oracle.jdbc.driver.OracleDriver
    </param-value>
  </init-param>
</servlet>
```

Score: _____

Notes: _____

_____

14. You have an initialization parameter defined in the deployment descriptor (web.xml) for a servlet. How would you retrieve the value of a parameter named "jdbcClassDriver"?

Skill Level: Intermediate

Expected answer:

You would use the: ServletConfig.getInitParameter("paramName") method as shown in the following example:

```
String jdbcClassDriver =
    getServletConfig().getInitParameter(
        "jdbcClassDriver");
```

Score: _____

Notes: _____

_____

15. You have a servlet where you need to retrieve several servlet initialization parameters from the deployment descriptor. Which method would be best to retrieve the names and values from so that they are only retrieved once, set in a variable global for the servlet? Keep in mind that this is a method that is already being passed the ServletConfig object?

Skill Level: Intermediate

Expected answer:

You would perform the parameter retrieval within the init method of the servlet.

Score: _____

Notes: _____

_____

16. Which method gets called by the servlet container immediately after the servlet is removed from service?

Skill Level: Low

Expected answer:

The destroy method is called.

Score: _____

Notes: _____

_____

17. A web application is a collection of JSP, servlet, HTML, image, JavaBeans, tag libraries, and other class files and libraries. Which object is created and maintained by the servlet container and contains all *context information* about your web application as a whole?

Skill Level: High

Expected answer:

A ServletContext object.

Score: _____

Notes: _____

_____

18. What are context-initialization parameters and how do they different from servlet-initialization parameters?

Skill Level: Low

Expected answer:

Context-initialization parameters (name/value pairs) are those that are defined for the entire context of the application within the web deployment descriptor file. They are said as having *application* scope. This differs from servlet-initialization parameters (again, name/value pairs) that are scoped at the servlet level. They are defined at the servlet level.

Score: _____

Notes: _____

_____

19. What is the name of the XML element used to store context-initialization parameters and which element do they need to be nested in within the web deployment descriptor file?

Skill Level: Intermediate

Expected answer:

Context-initialization parameters are defined in the web deployment descriptor using the <context-param> XML element. They are nested within the root element of the deployment descriptor; <web-app>.

Score: _____

Notes: _____

_____

20. What are the two types of listeners used in a Web application?

Skill Level: Intermediate

Expected answer:

Context attribute listeners and session attribute listeners.

Score: _____

Notes: _____

_____

21. Which interface, defined in the javax.servlet package, needs to be implemented to receive notifications about changes to the servlet context of the web application they are part of? *(For example when servlets are initialized or destroyed)*

Skill Level: High

Expected answer:

The ServletContextListener interface.

Score: _____

Notes: _____

_____

22. Which two methods would you need to implement within the ServletContextListener interface in order to handle the initializing and destroying of a servlet?

Skill Level: High

Expected answer:

The ServletContextListener interface has two methods that need to be implemented in order to handle the events when the web container creates and destroys a servlet:

```
contextInitialized(ServletContextEvent e);
contextDestroyed(ServletContextEvent e):
```

Score: _____

Notes: _____

_____

23. You want to override the attributeAdded method to handle the event of when an attribute is added to a session. Which interface would you find this method in?

Skill Level: High

Expected answer:

The attributeAdded method is defined in the HttpSessionAttributeListener interface.

Score: _____

Notes: _____

_____

24. You are writing a listener to enable you to listen for the notification from the servlet container that a session is being created. What is the name of the interface to implement and the method you need to override to accomplish this?

Skill Level: High

Expected answer:

The name of the interface is javax.servlet.http.HttpSessionListener and the name of the method to override is named sessionCreated.

Score: _____

Notes: _____

_____

25. What is the XML element name and syntax for defining a
servlet context listener?

Skill Level: High

Expected answer:
```
<listener>
  <listener-class>
    fully_qualified_class_name
  </listener-class>
</listener>
```

Score: _____

Notes: _____

_____

26. You are writing a servlet that is not thread safe. You would
like to have the servlet container execute your servlet by only
one thread at a time. Which interface would you implement to
make this happen?

Skill Level: Intermediate

Expected answer:
Have your servlet implement the SingleThreadModel. This
will tell the servlet container to not allow multiple threads
to access the servlet's methods simultaneously.

Score: _____

Notes: _____

_____

27. While writing a servlet, you want to write a message out the log file of the web application. What code would you write to log the string "Error Message" to the log file defined by the servlet container?

Skill Level: Intermediate

Expected answer:
```
ServletContext context = getServletContext();
String errorMessage = "Error Message";
context.log(errorMessage);
```

Score: _____

Notes: _____

_____

28. What is the signature of the method of the ServeltContext interface that allows the developer to log a string method and an exception to the log file?

Skill Level: Intermediate

Expected answer:
```
public void log(
          String message
      , Throwable throwable)
```

NOTE: The following signature has been depreciated in favor of the above one:

```
public void log(
          Exception exception
        , String msg)
```

Score: _____

Notes: _____

_____

29. You are developing a servlet that must retain sessions but the policy within the company prohibits cookies being turned on within the browser. Which two methods are available to allow you to put the session ID in the URL?

Skill Level: Intermediate

Expected answer:
```
encodeURL();
encodeRedirectURL();
```

Score: _____

Notes: _____

_____

30. What is the name of the parameter that stores the session ID of a servlet?

Skill Level: Intermedaite

Expected answer:
jsessionid

Score: _____

Notes: _____

_____

Java Server Pages (JSP)

1. JSP are not directly handled by the application container. What are JSPs converted to so they can be handled by the web application container?

    Skill Level: Low

    Expected answer:

    JSPs are converted to servlets.

    Score: _____

    Notes: _____

    _____

2. Are you supposed to put JSP files in the same directory where Java servlets are stored?

    Skill Level: Low

    Expected answer:

    No. JSP files along with any other static pages (i.e. HTML files) that are to be called directly should be put in the application root directory for the application.

    Score: _____

    Notes: _____

    _____

3. Briefly describe the lifecycle of a JSP?

    Skill Level: Intermediate

Expected answer:

- **Translate the page**. All tags are converted to Java source code – a servlet.

- **Compile the page**. The Java source code (servlet) is compiled into a class file.

- **Lode the class**. The servlet class gets loaded on its first request from a user.

- **Create an instance of the class**. The servlet container creates an instance of the class.

- **Make call to jspinit**. The servlet container will initialize the servlet instance by calling its jspinit method.

- **Make a call to _jspService**. The servlet container will then make a call to the _jspService method while passing in a *request* and *response* object.

- **Make a call to jspDestroy**. When the container needs to remove the JSP page from service, it will call the jspDestroy method.

Score: _____

Notes: _____

_____

4. Why is the response to a JSP file always slow for the first client request?

Skill Level: Intermediate

Expected answer:

When the JSP page is first called, it must go through a *translate* and *compile* stage which can be resource intensive. After it is converted to a servlet, the loads are very quick.

Score: _____

Notes: _____

_____

5. Within a JSP page, you need to declare and initialize a String object named *database* to the value of *"Oracle"*. How would you accomplish this?

Skill Level: Low

Expected answer:
```
<%! String database = new String ("Oracle"); %>
```

Score: _____

Notes: _____

_____

6. What are the two types of comments that can be put into a JSP page?

Skill Level: Low

Expected answer:
```
HTML comment: <!-- comment -->
JSP comment:  <%-- comment --%>
```

Score: _____

Notes: _____

_____

7. Within a JSP page, you have access to several objects that are implicitly declared. One of those objects is the response object. What are some of the things you can do with this object?

Skill Level: High

Expected answer:

You can use the response object to perform the following:

- Add cookies
- Return an error page
- Add a header
- Redirect the browser to another URL
- Set the HTTP status

Score: _____

Notes: _____

_____

8. How do you *import* other Java class files into your JSP page, just as you would do in a normal Java program?

Skill Level: Low

Expected answer:

You would use the import directive as shown in the following example:

```
<%@ page import="java.util.*;java.sql.*" %>
```

Score: _____

Notes: _____

_____

9. If you have a JSP page that must retain the session of each client, what directive would you set to inform the translation step to instantiate an HttpSession object?

Skill Level: Intermediate

Expected answer:

At the page level, you would set the session attribute to *true* as shown in the following example:

```
<%@ page session="true" %>
```

Score: _____

Notes: _____

_____

10. What is the default value for the session attribute in a JSP page?

Skill Level: Low

Expected answer:

True. If you do not session tracking, you would have to set the session attribute to false:

```
<%@ page session="false" %>
```

Score: _____

Notes: _____

_____

11. In a JSP file, how do you include the contents (source code) of another JSP into your code?

Skill Level: Low

Expected answer:

You would use the include directive as shown in the following example:

```
<%@ include file="myOtherJspFile" %>
```

Score: _____

Notes: _____

_____

12. You have a JavaBean named "com.acme.myBean" that you would like to declare and use in a JSP file. The bean should be scoped for the *page* and the object to be named "myBean". What is the syntax to perform this?

Skill Level: Low

Expected answer:

```
<jsp:useBean
    id="myBean"
    scope="page"
    class="com.acme.myBean"
/>
```

Score: _____

Notes: _____

_____

13. You are using a JavaBean within a JSP and want this same bean object to be shared by different users. What would you set the scope attribute to when declaring the bean in order to allow this?

Skill Level: Intermediate

Expected answer:

You would need to specify the scope attribute as "application" as shown in the following example:

```
<jsp:useBean
    id="myBean"
    scope="application"
    class="com.acme.myBean"
/>
```

Score: _____

Notes: _____

_____

14. You have a JavaBean declared in your JSP page that is named with the ID = "myBean". How would you retrieve the attribute named "amount" from this object given a correctly defined JavaBean?

Skill Level: Low

Expected answer:

Use the following syntax:

```
<jsp:getProperty
    name="myBean"
    property="amount"
/>
```

Score: _____

Notes: _____

_____

15. Which file contains the instructions to the container on where to find tab libraries by mapping a custom tag library URI to the actual tag library file?

Skill Level: Intermediate

Expected answer:

The web deployment descriptor file: web.xml.

Score: _____

Notes: _____

_____

16. You want to include a custom tag library in a JSP page. The URI for the library is "/myDBTagLibrary" and the tag prefix you want to use in your JSP page is "db". How would you write the tag library directive in your JSP page to perform this?

Skill Level: Intermedaite

Expected answer:
```
<%@ taglib
    uri="/myDBTagLibrary"
    prefix="db"
%>
```

Score: _____

Notes: _____

_____

17. When writing a tag handler Java class, which class do you need to extend?

Skill Level: High

Expected answer:
> javax.servlet.jsp.tagext.TagSupport

Score: _____

Notes: _____

_____

18. You have just coded and compiled a tag handler Java class to service custom tags in your JSP. Where do you put the tag handler classes?

Skill Level: Intermediate

Expected answer:
> The tag handler Java classes should be places in the WEB-INF/classes directory of your web application.

Score: _____

Notes: _____

_____

19. You have a JSP page that is not thread safe. What directive would you set to indicate this in your JSP page?

Skill Level: Intermediate

Expected answer:

You would set the isThreadSafe attribute to false as shown in the following example:

```
<%@ page isThreadSafe="false" %>
```

Score: _____

Notes: _____

_____

20. How do you declare in a JSP page that it should use an error page named "appError.jsp"?

Skill Level: Intermediate

Expected answer:

You would use the following:

```
<%@ page errorPage="appError.jsp" %>
```

Score: _____

Notes: _____

_____

Java Beans

1. What is a JavaBean?

Skill Level: Low

Expected answer:

A JavaBean is specification developed by Sun Microsystems that defines how Java objects interact. Specifically, they are reusable software components written in the Java programming language, designed to be manipulated visually by a software development environment (IDE), like JBuilder, Visual Age for Java, or JDeveloper – basically any application that understands the JavaBeans format.. JavaBeans are very similar to Microsoft's ActiveX components, but designed to be platform-neutral; running anywhere there is a Java Virtual Machine (JVM). JavaBeans can be dropped into an application container, (i.e. a form), and can then be used to perform functions ranging from a simple animation to complex calculations.

Score: _____

Notes: _____

_____

2. How do JavaBeans differ from Enterprise JavaBeans?

Skill Level: Intermediate

Expected answer:

The JavaBeans architecture is meant to provide a format for general-purpose components within a Java application. They are basically used to *"customize existing objects"*. Think about a button on a form that, when pressed, does not remain pressed – it bounces back to its off state, like a door-bell. The button acts as a single-state switch. Now you have to create a button that should have two stable states – like a typical light switch. In this case, you can take the existing button (the one having only one stable state) and "customize" it so that it has two stable states.

The Enterprise Java Beans (EJB) architecture, on the other hand, provides a format for highly specialized business (distributed) logic components. It is a completely distinctive concept than the one just mentioned above. EJB's are not used to customize an existing object. Instead they are used to "standardize" the way, in which business logic is written. For example, it is possible to write our business logic within the GUI logic, and also inside Servlets, Applets, and Standalone applications. Unfortunately, there is no clear distinction between the code that is responsible for the GUI and the actual business logic code, because all of the code is written inside the same class files. There is no chance for code reuse. By using EJBs, we can "componentize" the application by writing the business logic into separate class files than the GUI logic. This makes a clear distinction between the responsibilities of the GUI logic and the business logic.

Score: _____

Notes: _____

_____

3. What type of constructor is required for a class to be considered a JavaBean?

Skill Level: Low

Expected answer:

It must have a "no-arg" constructor.

Score: _____

Notes: _____

_____

4. What are the four requirements of a Java class to be considered a JavaBean?

Skill Level: Intermediate

Expected answer:

- The class must contain a no-arg constructor.

- The class will use standardized method names (getter/setter method naming paradigm) for property assessors and mutators.

- There are no public instance variables.

- The class must be public.

Score: _____

Notes: _____

_____

5. You want to include a JavaBean in a JSP page. Which three attributes should be supplied?

Skill Level: Intermediate

Expected answer:

- An ID – which provides a local name for the bean

- The Bean's Class Name – which is used to instantiate the bean if it does not exit

- A Scope – which specifies the lifetime of the bean, which by default is "page"

Score: _____

Notes: _____

_____

6. What would the syntax be if you wanted to include a JavaBean in a JSP with the following attributes:

ID   = "myBean"
Class = "com.acme.MyBean"
Scope = "session"

Skill Level: Low

Expected answer:
```
<jsp:useBean
    id="myBean"
    class="com.mycompany.MyBean"
    scope="session"
/>
```

Score: _____

Notes: _____

_____

7. What are the possible values for the "scope" attribute when initiating a JavaBean within a JSP document using the jsp:useBean action? What is the default value?

Skill Level: Intermediate

Expected answer:

The scope attribute defines the scope within which the reference is available. The possible values are **page**, **request**, **session**, and **application**. The default for the scope attribute is **page**.

Score: _____

Notes: _____

_____

8. You are using a JavaBean in a JSP and want to provide initial values when the bean gets created. How do you perform this?

Skill Level: High

Expected answer:

You would put the initialization code in the body of the jsp:useBean action tag. The body will not be executed if the bean already exists. Let's look at an example that utilizes the values used in the previous question:

```
<jsp:useBean id="myBean"
        class="com.mycompany.MyBean"
        scope="session">

<%-- this body is executed only if the
    bean is created. Now let's
    initialize some of the bean
    properties. --%>
<jsp:setProperty name="myBean"
            property="prop1"
```

```
                                 value="123" />
        </jsp:useBean>
```

Score: _____

Notes: _____

_____

9. You have included and initiated a JavaBean in a JSP named
   "myBean". What is the syntax of the action to perform in
   order to print the value of the property "prop1" to the
   generated output?

   Skill Level: Low

   Expected answer:
```
   <jsp:getProperty  name="myBean"
                     property="prop1">
```

Score: _____

Notes: _____

_____

10. When you include a JavaBean in a JSP using the jsp:useBean
    action, it declares a local Java variable to hold the bean object.
    What is the local Java variable name that it creates?

    Skill Level: Intermediate

    Expected answer:
    The name of the local Java variable that gets created from
    the jsp:useBean action is exactly the value of the ID
    attribute. In the action below, a local Java variable named
    "useBean" will be created.

```
<jsp:useBean
    id="myBean"
    class="com.mycompany.MyBean"
    scope="session"
/>
```

Score: _____

Notes: _____

_____

Design Patterns

1. What are Design Patterns?

   Skill Level: Low

   Expected answer:

   Design Patterns are expert solutions or descriptions to recurring software design problems in a given context. They are used to bring together the documentation and core solutions to communicate a given problem and its solution in software design. Design patterns are identified and documented in a form that is easy to distribute, discuss, and understand.

   Score: _____

   Notes: _____

   _____

2. What are some of the benefits of using Design Patterns in Java / J2EE?

   Skill Level: Intermediate

   Expected answer:

   - It is at the core of writing elegant and maintainable code.

   - Improve your system design.

   - Provides for a common vocabulary in discussing and design issues.

   - Provides for the ability to leverage proven and well tested solutions. Most of the common patterns have had many experts around the world testing and proving the solution to the problem.

- Promote design reuse and prevent reinventing the wheel.

- Provide solutions that can be applied to real-world problems.

- Promote class separation. Attempt to keep classes separated and prevent them from having to know too much information about one another.

- Allows you to work better with technologies like J2EE (designing EJBs, Servlets, JSPs, and JMS).

- Patterns can often be used together to solve a much larger problem.

- Can unveil bad practices in existing code or patterns that do not work. An in-depth understanding of design patterns allows the developer to easily refractor code and other design patterns to better solutions.

Score: _____

Notes: _____

_____

3. Most design patterns can be broken into three different types (or categories) of patterns. What are they and briefly describe each of them and their intended benefits?

Skill Level: Intermediate

Expected answer:

- **Creational** – These patterns are concerned with creating object instances for you, rather than having you instantiate objects directly. They allow your programs to be more flexible in deciding which objects need to be created for a given case and not require hard-coding.

- **Structural** – These patterns are concerned with the composition of objects. They allow developers to compose groups of objects into larger structures, such as complex user interfaces or accounting data.

- **Behavioral** – These patterns are concerned with the interaction and responsibility of objects. They assist the developer in defining communication between objects in a system and how the flow is controlled in a complex program.

Score: _____

Notes: _____

_____

4. What design pattern does the Struts framework adhere to?

Skill Level: Low

Expected answer:

The Struts application framework adheres to the MVC design pattern. This framework is used when development web components consisting of JSPs and servlets.

Score: _____

Notes: _____

_____

5. Briefly describe the Abstract Factory Method including its intent?

Skill Level: Intermediate

Expected answer:

The Abstract Factory Method provides in interface used to create and return families of related or dependent objects without actually specifying their concrete class. This pattern is used when you want to return one of several related classes of objects, each of which can return several different objects on request. It is often helpful to think of the Abstract Factory as a pattern as a factory object that returns one of several other factories.

Score: _____

Notes: _____

_____

6. What is a Session Facade?

Skill Level: High

Expected answer:

A Session Facade is a pattern commonly used when developing enterprise applications with the intent of defining a higher-level business component that contains and centralizes complex interactions between lower-level business components (i.e. Entity beans and other session beans). A Session Facade is implemented as a session enterprise bean and provides clients with a single interface for the functionality of an application or application subset. They also allow the developer to decouple lower-level business components from one another, making the system design more flexible and comprehensible.

Think about a banking application that has the option of allowing a customer to transfer a balance from one account to another. Visualize the application (client) as needing to check if the user is authorized, get the status of both accounts, check that there is enough money in the first account, and then finally perform the transfer of funds. This all needs to take place in a single transaction – if something goes wrong, the transaction need to be rolled back. As you can see, there can be multiple server side components (EJBs) that need to be accessed / modified. All of these invocations from the client can cause a tremendous amount of network traffic, poor reusability, high coupling, code maintainability, and performance problems because of the high latency of the remote calls from the client. Using a Session Facade design pattern, you can wrap all of the calls (invocations) into a single Session Bean, so the client will have a single point to access (that is the session bean) that will take care of handling all the rest.

Score: _____

Notes: _____

_____

7. What is a Singleton and why would you use this design pattern?

Skill Level: Intermediate

Expected answer:

The Singleton design pattern one of the "creational patterns" and is intended to ensure that a class has only one instance and also provides for a global point to access it from. Many applications that have only one window manager or print spooler or a single point of access to a relational database may need to prevent from having multiple instances.

Score: _____

Notes: _____

_____

8. What is the Iterator Design Pattern?

Skill Level: Low

Expected answer:

Probably one of the easiest and most widely used, the Iterator design pattern allows you to move through (access) a group of elements of an aggregate object (i.e. a list of collection) using a standard interface without having to know the details of its underlying implementation or the internal representations of the data. The developer can also create special iterators that perform some special processing (filtering) to only return specified elements of a data collection.

Score: _____

Notes: _____

_____

9. What are the two J2SE APIs associated with the Iterator design pattern?

Skill Level: Low

Expected answer:
```
java.util.Iterator
java.util.Enumeration
```

Score: _____

Notes: _____

_____

10. Which two packages in J2SE includes the Decorator pattern?

Skill Level: High

Expected answer:

The Decorator pattern is actually found in two different packages: java.io and java.awt.

Score: _____

Notes: _____

_____

11. What design pattern would you use as an alternative to sub-classing when you need to extend the functionality of an object dynamically?

Skill Level: High

Expected answer:

You could use the Decorator design pattern. The Decorator uses composition rather than inheritance to extend the functionality of an object during runtime.

Score: _____

Notes: _____

_____

12. You have a situation where you need to make a change to an object that requires making changes to other objects, and the number of objects that need to be changed are not known. The object needs to *notify* all other required objects but cannot make any assumptions about the identity of those objects. Which design pattern would you use?

Skill Level: High

Expected answer:

In this situation, it would be best to use the Observer design pattern. This design pattern defines a "one-to-many" dependency that provides for the ability to have all of its children objects notified and changed automatically when the parent is changed.

Score: _____

Notes: _____

_____

13. You have an application that uses a significant amount of objects. What design patter would you use if the resource cost are high because of the number of objects and you do not care about the identity of the object?

Skill Level: High

Expected answer:

The proper design pattern to use would be the Flyweight design pattern.

Score: _____

Notes: _____

_____

14. Consider an application that has to create a complex object and requires an algorithm that can create this object without being dependent on the components that comprise the object and how they are assembled. Which design patter would be most appropriate for this?

Skill Level: High

Expected answer:

The Builder Design Pattern.

Score: _____

Notes: _____

_____

15. What are the methods defined in the Iterator class?

Skill Level: Intermediate

Expected answer:
```
hasNext()
next()
remove()
```

Score: _____

Notes: _____

_____

Enterprise Java Beans (EJB)

1. What is an Enterprise Java Bean?

    Skill Level: Low

    Expected answer:

    > An Enterprise Java Bean (EJB) is component based architecture within the J2EE APIs that is used for developing and deploying component-based distributed business (enterprise) applications. It should contain the business logic for an application and is the heart of most J2EE applications.

    Score: _____

    Notes: _____

    _____

2. What are the three types of EJBs defined in the J2EE specification?

    Skill Level: Low

    Expected answer:

    - Session Bean
    - Entity Bean
    - Message-Driven Bean

Score: _____

Notes: _____

_____

3. You are tasked with writing an EJB that needs to act as a listener for the Java Messaging Service API and processes message asynchronously. Which type of EJB would you create?

Skill Level: Low

Expected answer:

A message-driven bean.

Score: _____

Notes: _____

_____

4. For an EJB, which software component provides for its transaction management, resource pooling, transaction management, and security checks?

Skill Level: Low

Expected answer:

An EJB container, which is one of the components of a J2EE application server.

Score: _____

Notes: _____

_____

5. What are some of the J2EE APIs an EJB container must support?

Skill Level: Low

Expected answer:

J2SE, JNDI, JMS, JavaMail, JAF, RMI-IIOP, JTA, JAAS, and JDBC.

Score: _____

Notes: _____

_____

6. What are the three class/interfaces that every EJB must have coded, as defined in the J2EE specification?

Skill Level: Intermediate

Expected answer:

- Home Interface
- Remote Interface
- The Bean Class (Session or Entity Bean)

Score: _____

Notes: _____

_____

7. You are developing a Session Bean and have already coded the *Home* and *Remote* interface and are now developing the Java Bean class. Which interface do you have to implement in the session bean class?

Skill Level: Intermediate

Expected answer:
```
javax.ejb.SesionBean
```

Score: _____

Notes: _____

_____

8. Which kind of methods go into the remote interface for an EJB?

Skill Level: Intermediate

Expected answer:
The remote interface is developed by the bean developer and should contain the business methods that can be called by the client. The remote interface actually acts as a proxy.

Score: _____

Notes: _____

_____

9. When developing the remote interface, which interface much it extend?

Skill Level: Low

Expected answer:

The remote interface should extend the javax.ejb.EJBObject interface.

Score: _____

Notes: _____

_____

10. When developing the Home interface, which interface much it extend?

Skill Level: Low

Expected answer:

The home interface should extend the javax.ejb.EJBHome interface.

Score: _____

Notes: _____

_____

11. What is the purpose of the Home interface in an EJB?

Skill Level: Low

Expected answer:

The home interface acts as a factory pattern and defines the methods that allow the client to create instances of the EJB as well as finding or removing an entity bean.

Score: _____

Notes: _____

_____

12. What are the two types of Session Beans?

Skill Level: Low

Expected answer:

- Stateless Session Beans
- Stateful Session Beans

Score: _____

Notes: _____

_____

13. What is the difference between a stateful session bean and a stateless session bean?

Skill Level: Intermediate

Expected answer:

A *stateless bean* does not hold any conversational state for a calling client's session. It is important to understand that technically, a stateless bean "may" hold state, but it is not guaranteed to be specific to the calling client. A stateless bean is appropriate for application business logic that does not need to hold the value of its instance variables for a client.

A *stateful bean*, on the other hand, is designed to retain its state for the duration of the client-bean session. The state of an object retained by the values of its instance variables. The instance variables are what represent the state of a unique client-bean session. When the client terminates (or removes) the bean, the session ends and its state no longer exists.

Score: _____

Notes: _____

_____

14. You need to write an EJB that must permanently persist data to a secondary storage device. Which type of bean would be most appropriate for this type of application?

Skill Level: Low

Expected answer:
   An entity bean.

   Score: _____

   Notes: _____

   _____

15. What is the purpose of Passivation of an EJB?

Skill Level: High

Expected answer:
   Passivation is a resource management technique to help in reducing the number if bean instances running on the system in order to conserve memory. The container will write the state of a bean to the filesystem in order for the instance of the bean to be used by another session.

   Score: _____

   Notes: _____

   _____

16. Passivation is only available with which two types of beans?

Skill Level: Intermediate

Expected answer*:*

Entity beans and stateful session beans.

Score: _____

Notes: _____

_____

17. Is it a requirement that an entity bean have a unique object identifier? If yes, then what is this unique identifier commonly called?

Skill Level: Low

Expected answer*:*

Yes. Each entity bean must have a unique object identifier. This unique identifier is commonly called the bean's *primary key*.

Score: _____

Notes: _____

_____

18. What is the difference between container-managed and bean-managed persistence? Which type of EJB does this refer to?

Skill Level: Low

Expected answer*:*

Let's first answer the second question – the idea of managed persistence refers to *entity beans*.

With *container-managed persistence*, the EJB container is responsible for saving the state of the bean. The bean's code will contain no database access code (SQL) to manage its state. The fields required for container-managed storage need to be specified in the deployment descriptor and the persistence is handled automatically by the container.

Bean-managed persistence, on the other hand, requires the developer of the entity bean to write the database access calls (SQL) code to retain its own state. The container will not generate any database code to assist in saving the state of the entity bean. This type of implementation is obviously less adaptable than container-managed persistence and needs to be hand-coded into the bean by the developer.

Score: _____

Notes: _____

_____

19. Why would you use bean pooling?

Skill Level: Intermediate

Expected answer:
EJBs are heavyweight components that require considerable system resources to create and destroy. It is advantageous for the container to manage a pool of EJBs that users will be able to use throughout the entire application. By having a bean pool in place, the container will be able to handle more user requests since it will not be wasting time and resources creating and destroying

objects. The pool of beans will be shared in an efficient way by all users of the system.

Score: _____

Notes: _____

_____

20. You have to write a bean that is involved with mostly workflow of a system and you need to use the lightest weight EJB, which type of bean would you choose?

Skill Level: Intermediate

Expected answer:

A stateless session bean.

Score: _____

Notes: _____

_____

21. Can a single message-driven bean instance process messages from multiple clients?

Skill Level: Intermediate

Expected answer:

Yes. All instances of a bean are equivalent. This allows the bean container to assign a message to any message-driven bean instance.

Score: _____

Notes: _____

_____

22. Does a message-driven bean's instance retain any data or conversational state for a specific client?

Skill Level: Intermediate

Expected answer:
No.

Score: _____

Notes: _____

_____

23. What are the only types of messages that can be processed by a message-driven bean as of the 1.3 release of the J2EE specification?

Skill Level: Low

Expected answer:
Message-driven beans can only process JMS messages. This may change in future release to process other kinds of messages.

Score: _____

Notes: _____

_____

24. What is the name and type of file used for an EJB deployment descriptor?

Skill Level: Low

Expected answer:

An XML file named ejb-jar.xml.

Score: _____

Notes: _____

_____

25. What is the root element in an EJB deployment descriptor?

Skill Level: Intermediate

Expected answer:

<ejb-jar>. All other elements must be nest within the <ejb-jar> tag.

Score: _____

Notes: _____

_____

26. Consider a Container-managed bean that has data that needs to be compressed or reformatted before saving to the database. Which method will the container call to perform this action before saving?

Skill Level: High

Expected answer:

The ejbStore method is called by the container before saving to the database for the purpose of compressing or reformatting.

Score: _____

Notes: _____

_____

27. You have a transactional client attempting to invoke an EJB method whose transactional attribute is set to 'NEVER' within a transaction context. What will happen?

Skill Level: High

Expected answer:

A RemoteException is thrown to the calling client. Setting the transactional attribute of an EJB method to 'NEVER' means that the bean method should never be invoked within the scope of a transaction.

Score: _____

Notes: _____

_____

28. Within the lifecycle of a stateless session bean, how many times does the ejbRemove method get invoked?

Skill Level: Low

Expected answer:
Only once.

Score: _____

Notes: _____

_____

29. To access an entity bean, which class is used to lookup the home object of an enterprise bean?

Skill Level: Intermediate

Expected answer:
The InitialContext class. When accessing an entity bean, the client needs to start a JNDI connection to obtain a directory connection to the bean's container. Once this connection is established, you will then create an InitialContext object. This object is then used to lookup the bean.

Score: _____

Notes: _____

_____

Java Message Service (JMS)

1. What is the Java Messaging Service (JMS)?

   Skill Level: Low

   Expected answer*:*
      The Java Messaging Service (JMS) is a J2EE service that enables support to exchange messages between Java programs. This allows applications can create, send, receive, and read messages. JMS provides support for asynchronous communication in Java. The sender and receiver do not have to know anything about each other – both the sender and receiver can operate independently.

   Score: _____

   Notes: _____

   _____

2. Which package would you find the JMS APIs?

   Skill Level: Low

   Expected answer:
      javax.jms

   Score: _____

   Notes: _____

   _____

3. Why would you choose messaging over other Java technologies like Remote Method Invocation (RMI) in an application?

Skill Level: Intermediate

Expected answer:

Java Messaging Service (JMS) is a very "loosely coupled" technology while RMI is a very "tightly coupled" technology.

You may have an application where the provider does not want the components to depend on information about other components' interfaces, so that application components can be easily swapped out.

Also, the provider may want the application to run whether or not all components are up and running simultaneously.

Lastly, the application model may want to allow a component to send information (messages) to another component and to continue execution without receiving an immediate response.

Score: _____

Notes: _____

_____

4. Which type of Enterprise Java Bean (EJB) was introduced to allow J2EE applications to process messages asynchronously?

Skill Level: Low

Expected answer:

Message-Driven Bean.

Score: _____

Notes: _____

_____

5. What are the two different types of message domains (sometimes called messaging models) that are supported by the JMS specification?

Skill Level: Low

Expected answer:

[1] Point-to-point – (Queue) and [2] Publish-and-Subscribe – (Topic).

Score: _____

Notes: _____

_____

6. Briefly describe the two types of message domains (sometimes called messaging models) defined in the JMS specification. Try to explain any timing dependency differences between the two.

Skill Level: Low

Expected answer:

Point-to-point – (Queue):

Point-to-point is built around the concept of message queues, senders, and receivers. A *message producer* sends a message to a specific queue. A *message consumer* can attach itself (connect) to a queue and listen for messages. When a message arrives on the queue, the consumer removes it from the queue and responds to it. Each message can have only one consumer. There are no timing dependencies for a producer and receiver of a message. It is possible for a receiver to receive a message whether or not it was running when the producer sent the message. A message can be sent to just one queue and will be processed by just one consumer. When the consumer reads the message, it will acknowledge the successful processing of the message.

Publish-and-Subscribe – (Topic):

In a Publish-and-Subscribe message domain, producers send messages to a *topic*. All of the registered consumers for that topic can retrieve those messages. Using Publish-and-Subscribe, many consumers can receive the same message. The system will take care of distributing messages arriving from a topic's multiple publishers to its multiple subscribers. Keep in mind that publishers and subscribers have timing dependencies. An application that subscribes to a topic can only consume messages published "after" the client has created a subscription and the subscriber is active before that time.

Score: _____

Notes: _____

_____

7. With the Point-to-Point message domain, can a consumer filter messages it receives? How? Where does the filtering get performed?

Skill Level: High

Expected answer:

Yes. Consumers can filter messages by using a *Message Selector*. This is done using a SQL-92 grammar which allows a message consumer to specify the messages it is interested in. Message selectors will assign the work of filtering messages to the JMS provider rather than to the application.

A message selector is a String object that contains an expression based on a subset of the SQL-92 conditional expression syntax. The methods createReceiver, createSubscriber, and createDurableSubscriber each have a form that allows the developer to specify a message selector as an argument when you create a message consumer. The message consumer will then only receive messages whose headers and properties match the selector. Here are several examples:

```
phone LIKE '412'
price BETWEEN 50 AND 100
name IN('Jeff','Alex')
JMSType IS NOT NULL
```

Score: _____

Notes: _____

_____

8. When using a Message Selector, can it filter messages based on the contents of the message body?

Skill Level: Intermediate

Expected answer:

No. A message selector cannot select messages on the basis of the content of the message body – only based on the header and properties of the message.

Score: _____

Notes: _____

_____

9. The Publish-and-Subscriber messaging domain defines a timing constraint between publishers and subscribers, where the subscriber has to be active at the time a message is produced in order to receive it. How does the JMS API relax this timing dependency?

Skill Level: High

Expected answer:

The client can create a *durable subscription*. A durable subscription can receive messages sent even when the subscribers are not active. This allows for a messaging model that allows clients to send messages to many recipients without the timing constraints imposed by the default nature of publish-and-subscriber.

Score: _____

Notes: _____

_____

10. What are the three components of a Message?

Skill Level: Low

Expected answer:

- Header
- Properties
- Body

Score: _____

Notes: _____

_____

11. What kind of information is found in the header of a Message?

Skill Level: Intermediate

Expected answer:

The header of a message contains message identification and routing information. This includes, but is not limited to:

- JMSDestination
- JMSDeliveryMode
- JMSMessageID
- JMSTimeStamp
- JMSExpiration
- JMSReplyTo
- JMSCorrelationID

- JMSType
- JMSRedelivered

Score: _____

Notes: _____

_____

12. Describe the 5 message body formats (also called message types) defined in the JMS API?

Skill Level: Low

Expected answer:

- **StreamMessage**: A stream of primitive values in the Java that is filled and read sequentially.

- **MapMessage**: Holds a set of name/value pairs where the names are String's and the values are primitive types defined in Java. The entries can be read either sequentially by an enumerator or randomly by name. There is no order defined for this type of message.

- **BytesMessage**: A stream of non-interpreted bytes of type byte[]. Used for encoding a body to math an existing message format.

- **TextMessage**: A java.lang.String object. (i.e. an XML, CSV or HTML file)

- **ObjectMessage**: A serialized object. Of type Object.

Score: _____

Notes: _____

_____

13. You are about to create a QueueSession object (javax.jms.QueueSession). Which object is used to create a QueueSession object?

Skill Level: Intermediate

Expected answer:

A QueueSession object is created from a QueueConnection object as show in the following snippet:

```
queueConnection =
  queueConnectionFactory.createQueueConnection();

queueSession =
    queueConnection.createQueueSession(
        false
      , Session.AUTO_ACKNOWLEDGE
    );
```

Score: _____

Notes: _____

_____

14. What are some of the things a QueueSession is responsible for creating?

Skill Level: Intermediate

Expected answer:

- Messages
- Senders
- Receivers
- Transactions

Score: _____

Notes: _____

_____

15. You have a QueueSession object named queueSession and want to create a *Text Message Type* named textMessage. What would the syntax be?

Skill Level: Intermediate

Expected answer:
```
TextMessage message =
    queueSession.createTextMessage();
```

Score: _____

Notes: _____

_____

16. Is a QueueSession object single or multi-threaded?

Skill Level: Low

Expected answer:

Single threaded. Any message sending and receiving happens in a well-defined serial order.

Score: _____

Notes: _____

_____

17. You have a TextMessage object named message. How would you assign the content (body) of the message to "Test Message"?

Skill Level: Low

Expected answer:
```
TextMessage message =
    queueSession.createTextMessage();

message.setText("Test Message");
```

Score: _____

Notes: _____

_____

18. Message consumer clients can receive messages in two different way; blocking and non-blocking. What are the two methods of javax.jms.MessageConsumer used to receive messages in blocking and non-blocking mode?

Skill Level: Low

Expected answer:

Blocking mode: `receive()`
Non-blocking mode: `receiveNoWait()`

Score: _____

Notes: _____

_____

19. In the javax.jms.MessageConsumer class, what does the method receive(long) do?

Skill Level: Intermediate

Expected answer:

Notice that the receive method takes one argument – a Java long. This method will retrieve the next message that arrives within the specified timeout interval (defined by the value of the long passed in). This call will block until a message arrives, the timeout expires, or this message consumer is closed.

Score: _____

Notes: _____

_____

20. Given the method javax.jms.MessageConsumer.receive(long), what value would you pass so that the call will block indefinitely and never timeout?

Skill Level: High

Expected answer:

Pass in the value zero.

Score: _____

Notes: _____

_____

21. Describe the lifecycle of a JMS Sender application by explaining the steps you would need to perform in order to send a message.

Skill Level: Intermediate

Expected answer:

- Use the JNDI to get a ConnectionFactory and Destination object. (either Queue or Topic)
- Create a Connection object.
- Create a Session object in order for sending/receiver messages.
- Create a MessageProducer object. (either a TopicPublisher or QueueSender)
- Start the connection.
- Send (publish) the message to its destination.
- Close the session and connection.

Score: _____

Notes: _____

_____

22. Describe the lifecycle of a JMS Receiver application by explaining the steps you would need to perform in order to receive a message that will block?

Skill Level: Intermediate

Expected answer:

- Use the JNDI to get a ConnectionFactory and Destination object. (either Queue or Topic)

- Create a Connection object.

- Create a Session object in order for sending/receiver messages.

- Create a MessageConsumer object. (either a TopicSubscriber or QueueReceiver)

- Start the connection.

- Receive the message.

- Close the session and connection.

Score: _____

Notes: _____

_____

23. Messages are not considered successful until they have been acknowledged. What are the four types of acknowledgment?

Skill Level: High

Expected answer:

- **Acknowledgement by commit**. This is the only type allowed in a transacted sessions. In this case, acknowledgment happens automatically when a transaction is committed.

- **Session.AUTO_ACKNOWLEDGE**. Passed as the second argument to the createQueueSession method, the session will automatically acknowledge upon successful return from MessageConsumer.receive() or MessageListener.onMessage() method call.

- **Session.CLIENT_ACKNOWLEDGE**. Passed as the second argument to the createQueueSession method, the client must call the acknowledge() method of Message object.

- **Session.DUPS_OK_ACKNOWLEDGE**. Passed as the second argument to the createQueueSession method, this is sometimes referred to as early acknowledgement. It instructs the session to simply acknowledge the message after it has been delivered. This is likely to result in the delivery of some duplicate messages if the JMS provider fails. Consumers need to be able to tolerate duplicate messages.

Score: _____

Notes: _____

_____

24. As it relates to acknowledgement, what happens to messages if a transaction is rolled back?

Skill Level: Intermediate

Expected answer:

If a transaction is rolled back, all consumed messages are re-delivered.

Score: _____

Notes: _____

_____

25. Which J2EE service is used to manage distributed transactions in a JMS application?

Skill Level: Low

Expected answer:
Java Transaction API (JTA)

Score: _____

Notes: _____

_____

Non-Technical Questions

When conducting an on-site or telephone interview, it's very important that you be able to assess non-technical information about your job candidate. These non-technical factors include motivation, thinking skills, and personal attitude. All of these factors have a direct bearing on the ultimate success of the candidate in your shop, and also give you an idea about the longevity of a particular client.

Each of these questions is deliberately ambiguous and probing so that the job candidate will have an opportunity to speak freely. Often these questions will give you a very good idea of the suitability of the candidate for the position. Remember, in many IT shops technical ability is secondary to the ability of the candidate to function as a team member within the organization.

1. What are your plans if you don't get this job?

    This question can reveal a great deal about the motivation of the job candidate. If the candidate indicates that he/she will change career fields, going into an unrelated position, then this person may not have a long-term motivation to stay within the IT industry. If, on the other hand, the candidate responds that he will continue to pursue opportunities within the specific technical area, then the candidate is probably dedicated to the job for which he is being interviewed.

2. How do you feel about overtime?

    This is an especially loaded question, because any honest job candidate is going to tell you that they don't like to work overtime. As we know, the reality of today's IT world is that the professional will occasionally have to work evenings and weekends. This question is essential if you're interviewing for a position that requires non-traditional hours, such as a network administrator or database administrator, where the bulk of the production changes will occur on evenings, weekends, and holidays.

3. Describe your biggest non-technical flaw.

    This question provides insight into the personality of the job candidate, as well as their honesty and candor. Responses are unpredictable and may range from "I don't suffer fools gladly" to "I have a hard time thinking after I've been on the job for 16 hours". Again, there is no right or wrong answer to this question, but it may indicate how well the candidate is going to function during critical moments. More importantly, this question gives an idea of the level of self-awareness of the candidate, and gauges whether or not they are actively working to improve their non-technical skills.

4. Describe your least favorite boss or professor.

    The answer to this question will reveal the candidate's opinions and attitudes about being supervised by others. While there is no correct response to this question, it can shed a great deal of light on the candidates's interpersonal skills.

5. Where do you plan to be ten years from now?

    This is an especially important question for the IT job candidate because it reveals a lot about their motivations. As we know, the IT job industry does not have a lot of room for advancement within the technical arena, and someone who plans to rise within the IT organization will be required to move into management at some point. It's interesting that the response to this question is often made to be overly important, especially amongst those managers that hear the response in ten years I would like to have your job furious his there's a half

6. How important is money to you?

Again, this is an extremely misleading question, because even though many IT professionals deeply enjoy their jobs, and some would even do it for free, money is a primary motivator for people in the workplace. This question provides an easy opportunity to find out whether or not your candidate is being honest with you.

An appropriate answer for the candidate might be to say that he greatly enjoys his work within IT but that he needs to be able to maintain some level of income in order to support his family. A bonus benefit of this question is it also provides insight into the demographic structure of the job candidate, namely their marital status, as well as the age of their children, and whether or not they have immediate family in the area. Its well-known within the IT industry that job candidates are most likely to remain with the company if they have a large extended family group within the immediate area

7. Why did you leave your last job?

This is one of the most loaded questions of all, and one that can be extremely revealing about the personality of the IT job candidate. The most appropriate answer to this question is that the previous job was not technically challenging enough, or that the candidate was bored.

However, periodically you will find job candidates who will express negativity regarding the work environment, the quality of the management, and the personalities of the co-workers. This of course, should be a major red flag, because it may indicate that this job candidate does not possess the interpersonal skills required to succeed in a team environment.

8. If you were a vegetable, which vegetable would you be?

    On its face, this is a totally ludicrous and ambiguous question, but it gives you an opportunity to assess the creative thinking skills of the job candidate. For example, if the job candidate merely replies "I don't know", he may not possess the necessary creative thinking skills required for a systems analyst or developer position.

    A creative candidate will simply pick a vegetable, and describe in detail why that particular vegetable suits their personality. For example, the job candidate might say "I would be broccoli because I am health-oriented, have a bushy head, and go well with Chinese food".

9. Describe the month of June.

    The answer to this question also provides insight into the thinking ability of the job candidate. For example, most job candidates may reply that June is a summer month, with longer days, hot weather, and an ideal vacation time. The candidate with an engineering or scientific point of view might reply instead that June is a month with 30 days, immediately preceding the summer equinox.

10. Why do you want to work here?

    This is the candidate's opportunity to express why he might be a good fit for your particular organization. It also indicates whether the candidate has taken the time to research the company and the work environment. Is the candidate applying for this position solely because he needs a job, any job, or because he has specifically singled out your company due to some appealing characteristic of the work environment?

This question can also add information about the motivation of the job candidate, because a job candidate who is highly motivated to work for a particular firm will make the effort to research the company, the work environment, and even the backgrounds of individual managers.

Using a powerful search engine such as Google, the savvy IT candidate can quickly glean information about the person who is interviewing them. Having detailed knowledge of the organization is a very positive indicator that the candidate has given a lot of thought to the particular position and is evidence of high motivation.

General Questions

1. What do you know about our company?

   Answer: _____

   Comment: _____

   _____

If the prospective employee has little or no knowledge about the company, then he will also have little idea about how he can benefit the company. A candidate who has not gone to the trouble of researching the organization may be after a job, any job.

A candidate who has taken the time to explore the company will probably have specific ideas in mind about what he can bring to the organization. The initiative required by the candidate to research the company is a good sign that he is proactive and not passive dead weight.

If the candidate has some knowledge of the company's mission and function, this will also become apparent in the questions he asks you. He will already be thinking about how he can fit in and how his skills can be utilized, desirable traits of the problem-solver.

2. Why do you want to work for this company? Why should we hire you?

Answer: _____

Comment: _____

_____

The answer to this question can reveal whether the candidate is merely shopping for a job or has true interest in the company and the position. It is important that the candidate show some passion for the field, if he does not, he will probably never be creative in the work environment, and he will not represent a solution for you.

Does the candidate have a core belief that his particular set of skills can benefit you? Answers such as "I believe my experience can make a difference here", or "I believe your company will provide an environment that more directly engages my interest", or "Working for your company will provide challenges that excite me" are good starters.

3. Why are you looking for a new job?

Answer: _____

Comment: _____

_____

Typical reasons for seeking a new job include the desire to advance in the field and boredom in a job that offers few fresh challenges. These are positive motivations, but there can be negative ones as well. There may be personal conflicts between the candidate and other team members or management that have become so adversarial that the candidate is compelled to leave.

While not necessarily eliminating a candidate from consideration, personal friction in the previous job does raise a red flag. It may be that the candidate is an unfortunate victim of backroom politics, but if he confides in you about the shortcomings of his supervisors or fellow employees, while taking no responsibility himself, you must consider yourself warned.

4. Tell us about yourself / your background.

Answer: _____

Comment: _____

_____

This is probably asked more than any other question in interviews. It is the main opportunity for the candidate to describe his experiences, motivations, and vision of himself as it relates to the company.

The candidate should provide clear examples of how his abilities were used in the past to solve problems. If the candidate just repeats the information in the resume, he is probably only going through the motions and has no clear vision of his role in the company.

Even worse, if the candidate contradicts the resume, there is evidence of a serious problem.

5. What are the three major characteristics that you bring to the job?

Answer: _____

Comment: _____

_____

The candidate should offer specific skills or traits that he believes will be useful in the position. If the candidate is unable to relate these characteristics to the job, he has obviously not thought much about his role in the organization. You are interested in finding someone who has ideas about how he can hit the ground running and make a real difference to the company.

6. Describe the "ideal" job... the "ideal" supervisor.

Answer: _____

Comment: _____

_____

This question is not as open-ended as it may seem. If the candidate's ideal job has little or nothing in common with the position he is interviewing for, he is unlikely to be a good fit. The candidate's response should match fairly well with the requirements of the position.

The candidate's description of the ideal supervisor can provide clues about how well the candidate works with superiors. Beware the candidate who seizes this as an opportunity to denigrate past managers.

7. How would you handle a tough customer?

Answer: _____

Comment: _____

_____

Can the candidate provide examples of instances when difficult clients were won over? An effective communicator can strike a balance between meeting the needs of the customer and dealing with unrealistic expectations.

Above all, the candidate should indicate that he understands the necessity of "going the extra mile" to alleviate the concerns of the customer. Providing service to the client or end user is fundamental to the success of any enterprise.

8. How would you handle working with a difficult co-worker?

Answer: _____

Comment: _____

_____

This is similar to the last question. The candidate should relate an example of a conflict with a co-worker or team member that was successfully resolved. What you are looking for is evidence that the candidate is able to facilitate communication and lead a difficult project to a successful conclusion.

9. When would you be available to start if you were selected?

Answer: _____

Comment: _____

_____

There is obviously not right or wrong answer to this question. It merely gives you an indication as to the schedule you and the candidate need to work within.

10. How does this position match your career goals?

Answer: _____

Comment: _____

_____

This is an excellent question to ascertain whether the candidate truly sees the position as an integral part of his career path. Does the candidate believe the knowledge and experience he will gain from this job will move him to where he wants to be?

A thorough answer to this question will lead into the next one.

11. What are your career goals (a) 3 years from now; (b) 10 years from now?

Answer: _____

Comment: _____

_____

The answer to this question will indicate the level of commitment the candidate feels towards the job and the company. If the candidate has a goal in mind, how well does it fit with the job he is applying for?

When the candidate describes his goals, does he speak in terms of the skills and abilities he hopes to acquire that will prepare him for his eventual role, or does he simply want to be the CEO, with little thought of what it might take to get there?

The interviewer may be surprised by how often the candidate will talk about goals that are unrelated to the position.

12. What do you like to do in your spare time?

Answer: _____

Comment: _____

_____

This question provides an opportunity to learn more about the character of the candidate, and to judge whether his outside interests complement his professional life. Is the candidate well-rounded or one-dimensional? Does he tend to sustain an interest over time?

13. What motivates you to do a good job?

Answer: _____

Comment: _____

_____

If the candidate responds "making money" or "avoiding the wrath of my boss", you probably have a problem. The candidate should describe some positive motivation, such as a new challenge, and tie it to a specific example of a time in the past when the motivation reaped personal rewards and results on the job.

14. What two or three things are most important to you at work?

Answer: _____

Comment: _____

_____

The answer to this can reveal much about how the candidate sees himself on the job. Does the candidate mention things such as the importance of interpersonal communication, or responding quickly to crisis situations, things that facilitate job performance, or does he seem to be more worried about the timeliness of his coffee breaks?

15. What qualities do you think are essential to be successful in this kind of work?

Answer: _____

Comment: _____

_____

Does the candidate have a realistic idea of what the work environment requires of him, and do the qualities of the candidate match the job? Does the candidate have an example of a past job experience when these qualities were called upon with beneficial results?

16. How does your previous work experience prepare you for this position?

Answer: _____

Comment: _____

_____

This question relates to many of the others. If the candidate is able to articulate a clear idea of how his previous experience and training has prepared him for the responsibilities of the new position, he will be well ahead of many other interviewees.

17. How do you define "success"?

Answer: _____

Comment: _____

_____

If the answer doesn't fit the position, the candidate may be unhappy in the field, or quickly become bored. This indicates that the candidate may not be committed to staying with the company for very long.

18. What has been your most significant accomplishment to date?

Answer: _____

Comment: _____

_____

The candidate should be able to relate a specific example of an achievement that demonstrates a desirable quality for the job. The candidate should focus on action and results, rather than long-winded descriptions of situations.

The answer to this question can provide insight into situations that the candidate may handle especially well. The candidate should demonstrate an ability to persevere and overcome obstacles. Did the person deliver more than was expected of him in a difficult situation?

19. Describe a failure and how you dealt with it.

Answer: _____

Comment: _____

_____

This is known as a negative question, and it can be extremely revealing. It can indicate significant weaknesses or problems that may interfere with the ability to do the job.

Was the failure a catastrophic one, or a relatively minor problem? Was the candidate able to learn from the experience and apply the knowledge to future situations?

The answer to this question can also reveal how much personal accountability and responsibility the candidate accepts. If the candidate blames the failure on others, he is not likely to learn from his mistakes.

As with most interview questions, this questions is designed to provide insight into the overall personality of the candidate, and gives you a fuller appreciation of the strengths, as well as the weaknesses, of the person.

20. What leadership roles have you held?

Answer: _____

Comment: _____

_____

This answer should indicate not only that the candidate has the leadership experience to succeed in the new job, but that he has the ability to work well with others and is able to shoulder the responsibility and deal with the pressure associated with the requirements of the position.

21. Are you willing to travel?

Answer: _____

Comment: _____

_____

The answer here will demonstrate how committed to the company the candidate is likely to be. If the candidate dismisses the idea of travel completely, he may lack the motivation you are looking for.

22. What have you done in the past year to improve yourself?

Answer: _____

Comment: _____

_____

This question can shed more light on the personality of the candidate. If the candidate has been motivated by the goal of obtaining this position, he will be able to demonstrate that he has taken the initiative to prepare himself for it.

If the candidate instead chooses to describe the benefits of his basket-weaving class, he may indeed be the better for it, but it has little relevance to solving the problems he would soon encounter in the new position.

23. In what areas do you feel you need further education and training to be successful?

Answer: _____

Comment: _____

_____

If the answer has nothing to do with the offered position, the candidate may soon become bored. This question is similar to others and should dovetail with other answers about goals and career path.

24. What are your salary requirements?

Answer: _____

Comment: _____

_____

If the candidate mentions a figure that is too low, he may be uninformed or desperate. On the other hand, if his financial expectations are unreasonable, he should probably be eliminated from consideration.

The following questions are designed to zero in on key aspects of the candidate's personality and ability to perform. You may find it helpful to assign each response a score between 1 and 5 (a shorthand assessment technique that may also be used with many of the preceding questions).

Policies and Procedures

While technical expertise is essential in many IT positions, many interviews fall short in determining the discipline of a potential candidate. The questions in this section assist in determining if a potential candidate acts in accordance with established policies, procedures, and guidelines. Does he or she follow standard procedures even in crisis situations? Can they effectively communicate and enforce organizational policies and procedures along with recognizing and constructively conforming to unwritten rules?

1. Many jobs require employees to act in strict accordance with established policies. Describe to me a time when you were expected to act in accordance with policy even when it was not convenient or you disagreed with the policy. What did you do in this situation?

   > Was the candidate able to demonstrate their commitment to follow policy even if good reasons could have been made for breaking it? Look for any non-conformity to policy because of disrespect for those who made the policy, personal style, revenge, or dishonesty?

   Answer: _____

   Comment: _____

   _____

2. Many IT projects involve managing tasks and situations that involve potential for high money loss conditions. Describe a time when you have been asked to manage a situation like this and how you were able to ensure your job effectiveness.

Was the candidate able to demonstrate a "no exceptions" attitude and strategy that showed systematic and rigorous use of policy, guidelines and procedures to ensure consistency? In attempts to achieve consistency, did he or she show any "dislike" for the rules and preferences? Was there dislike for rules and preferences by the candidate for doing the job his or her way?

Answer: _____

Comment: _____

_____

3. Explain a time when you found a particular policy or procedure challenging or difficult to adhere to. How did you handle it?

Did the candidate take great pains to adhere to the policy and communicate the difficulty to proper management for review and/or revision? Was there an unnecessary risky deviation from policy, and no communication of either the challenge or deviation to management?

Answer: _____

Comment: _____

_____

Quality

This section provides questions that help in determining the quality of potential candidates. Does he or she maintain high standards despite pressing deadlines as well as establishing high standards and measures within the organization? Look for answers that demonstrate the candidate performs work correctly the first time and inspects material for potential flaws. You also want to know that they test new methods thoroughly and reinforce excellence as a fundamental priority.

1. Explain a situation in which an important deadline was nearing, but you didn't want to compromise quality. How did you deal with it and what was its outcome?

   Was the candidate able to maintain high quality through investing additional resources, moving deadlines, or making a statement of work in progress? Did he or she sacrifice quality, possibly resulting in additional problems at a later time? Did the situation result in a positive outcome?

   Answer: _____

   Comment: _____

   _____

2. Tell me about a situation or task you had to develop or coordinate that had to be exactly right. How did you test it and what was the outcome?

   Was the candidate able to rigorously identify potential sources of problems and systematically address them? Did he or she run ample trials to accurately satisfy the requirements? Look for possible problems, insufficient experimentation, or minimal piloting?

Answer: _____

Comment: _____

_____

3. Describe a situation or task you were responsible for where you made quality a fundamental priority within your organization. What steps did you take to do this?

Was the candidate able to demonstrate systematic approaches like correction systems, control systems, error prevention systems, or even implementing training? Look for problems with their approach like haphazard or inadequate support of quality functions?

Answer: _____

Comment: _____

_____

Commitment to Task

When determining a candidate's commitment to task, you need to verify their ability to take responsibility for actions and outcomes as well as their persistence despite obstacles. Will this employee be available around the clock in case of emergencies and be able to provide long hours to the job when needed. Ask questions that allow the candidate to demonstrate their dependability in difficult circumstances and if they show a sense of urgency about getting the job done.

1. Explain a difficult task or situation in which you took full responsibility for actions and outcomes. How did you act on this?

   Was the candidate able to publicly claim responsibility, and then cautiously manage the situation to a successful outcome? Did it involve other parties with divergent goals? Was he or she able to resolve the situation but still accepting responsibility?

   Answer: _____

   Comment: _____

   _____

2. There are people that can be counted on to go the extra mile when their company really needs it. Tell me about a time when you demonstrated dependability and reliability in trying circumstances.

   Was the candidate able to talk about situations or task where they worked long hours to perform unique job duties to help the organization get through a personnel shortage or demanding deadlines? Did the candidate put in "extra effort" and consistently demonstrate the notion that it was not the company's problem?

Answer: _____

Comment: _____

_____

3. Tell me about a time when you dedicated long hours to a job. For example, do you take work home, work on weekends or maintain long hours for system integrity or maintenance?

Was the candidate able to demonstrate self-direction and initiative in working particularly lengthy hours, with clear commitment to a meaningful objective? Ensure compliance to routine work requirements as well as no qualms about what was expected of them.

Answer: _____

Comment: _____

_____

4. Tell me about a time when you demonstrated a sense of urgency or importance about getting results.

Did the candidate demonstrate that they took immediate action directed toward a specific objective, so that non-task activities and interests were given a lower priority while productivity and efficiency were given top priority? Ensure they were able to clearly explain their emphasis on effectiveness, speed, and efficiency.

Answer: _____

Comment: _____

_____

Planning, Prioritizing and Goal Setting

Questions in this category demonstrate a candidate's ability to prepare for emerging customer needs, manage multiple projects, and determine project urgency in a meaningful and sensible way. Look for their use of goals to guide actions and create detailed action plans, organize and schedule tasks and people.

1. Tell me about a situation that explains how well you manage multiple projects at one time.

   > Was the candidate able to keep all projects moving at a pace to hit deadlines and in a systematic, manageable, quality way using a meaningful approach to prioritizing? Was there haphazard allotment of resources to different tasks, with unproductive and unnecessary chaos?

   Answer: _____

   Comment: _____

   _____

2. Many factors can help in setting meaningful priorities based on ease of task, customer size, deadlines, etc. Tell me about a time when it was challenging for you to prioritize.

   > Did the candidate use a sensible set of priorities and apply them consistently? Make sure that the candidate does not demonstrate excess bouncing of resources, resulting in inefficiencies, or a poor choice of criteria on which to prioritize.

Answer: _____

Comment: _____

_____

3. Describe a project in which you proficiently coordinated tasks, people, and schedules. How did you perform in this situation and what was the outcome?

Did the candidate use a systematic and concentrated approach to identify tasks, people who can perform the tasks, adjusting schedules, and project constraints? Ensure that their steps were not an overly simplistic approach that was inadequate given the complexities of the project.

Answer: _____

Comment: _____

_____

Attention to Detail

The questions in this section help to determine the candidate's ability to be "alert" in high-risk environments. Does he or she consistently follow detailed procedures and ensure accuracy in documentation and data. Do they carefully monitor reports, processes, system performance and concentrate on routine work details plus organize and maintain a system of records.

1. Explain a time when you were tasked to apply changes to a mission critical and potentially high money loss system. What steps did you take to insure the stability and integrity of the system? What procedures did you take to ensure a successful outcome and what were the results?

   Ensure the candidate dutifully monitored all potentially troublesome aspects of the environment, and addressed anything that was not perfect. Did the candidate take careful steps and remain aware of potential trouble spots, and not rely on subsequent quick reactions in favor of prevention?

   Answer: _____

   Comment: _____

   _____

2. Tell me about an experience from your past, which illustrates your ability to be attentive to details when monitoring a mission critical system. Explain the details of how you approached this and what were the results.

   Was the candidate able to demonstrate commitment to monitoring and understanding the system, and to using a well thought out strategy to ensure/enhance attention to detail? Also question that the candidate was not "overconfident" and giving little awareness of potential distractions.

Answer: _____

Comment: _____

_____

3. How do you go about ensuring accuracy and consistency in situations or tasks as in preparing a document or ensuring system integrity? Describe a specific case in which your attention to detail paid off.

   Was the candidate able to take clear and consistent precautions such as proofing thoroughly, double-checking, verifying format consistency, etc.? Was there only a cursory spot check or did they check and double-check accuracy?

   Answer: _____

   Comment: _____

   _____

4. Do you have problems in dealing with "routine work"? Describe your experiences in coping with routine work. What kinds of problems did you have to overcome in order to focus and concentrate on the details of the job?

   Was the candidate able to use strategic means to maintain attentiveness and focus during routine work? Did he or she show any diminished alertness, with little effort being made to remove or reduce it?

Answer: _____

Comment: _____

_____

5. Tell me about a situation or task that demonstrates your ability to organize and maintain a system of records.

Was the candidate able to initiate or illustrate commitment to a systematic method for organization and record keeping? Look for possible ineffectiveness record keeping, or overconfidence on human memory, or dependence on others?

Answer: _____

Comment: _____

_____

Self-Initiative

Self-initiative is a valuable asset in any employee. Questions in this category should test potential candidates by asking them about times when they undertook additional responsibilities and were able to respond to situations as they arose with no supervision. Does this candidate demonstrate the ability to bring about significant results from ordinary circumstances? Do they prepare for problems or opportunities in advance?

1. Describe to me a situation in which you assertively capitalized on an opportunity and converted something ordinary into something extraordinary?

    Was the candidate able to demonstrate a time when they took an ordinary and routine situation and were able to put forth a unique solution that yielded positive results. It should be a unique solution that may not have been achieved by others given the same situation? Was the outcome of the accomplishment of little magnitude or what would have been expected of anyone in that situation?

    Answer: _____

    Comment: _____

    _____

2. Describe a situation where you responded to a situation as it arose with little or no supervision.

    Was the candidate able to demonstrate a situation where they took reasonable, quick and decisive action given an appropriate amount of information or research, affirming their independence? Pay attention to their use of authority

– was it appropriate? Did the candidate make good decisions with little procrastination?

Answer: _____

Comment: _____

_____

3. Tell me about a time when you voluntarily took on a special project that was above and beyond your normal responsibilities.

Despite an already full workload, did the candidate still volunteer for a large or complex task? Where they able to successfully complete the task without undue compromise of other responsibilities? Verify the candidate did not unnecessarily sacrifice other areas of responsibilities.

Answer: _____

Comment: _____

_____

4. Many people contend to have good ideas, but so few act on them. Describe to me how you've transformed a good idea into a productive and beneficial business outcome.

Did the candidate produce an organized and meaningful action plan to bring their idea to fruition? Verify that the action plan was organized, realistic and productive.

Answer: _____

Comment: _____

_____

Index

M

O

P

Q

R

S

About Jeffrey Hunter

Jeffrey Hunter graduated from Stanislaus State University in Turlock California with a Bachelor's degree in Computer Science. Jeff is an Oracle Certified Professional, Java Development Certified Professional, and currently works as an independent Senior Database Administrator.

His work includes advanced performance tuning, Java programming, capacity planning, database security, and physical / logical database design in a UNIX, Linux, and Windows NT environment. Jeff's other interests include mathematical encryption theory, programming language processors (compilers and interpreters) in Java and C, LDAP, writing web-based database administration tools, Xemacs and of course Linux.

About Mike Reed

When he first started drawing, Mike Reed drew just to amuse himself. It wasn't long, though, before he knew he wanted to be an artist.

Today he does illustrations for children's books, magazines, catalogs, and ads.

He also teaches illustration at the College of Visual Art in St. Paul, Minnesota. Mike Reed says, "Making pictures is like acting — you can paint yourself into the action." He often paints on the computer, but he also draws in pen and ink and paints in acrylics. He feels that learning to draw well is the key to being a successful artist.

Mike is regarded as one of the nation's premier illustrators and has is the creator of the popular "Flame Warriors" illustrations at **www.flamewarriors.com**. A renowned children's artist, Mike has also provided the illustrations for dozens of children's books.

Mike Reed has always enjoyed reading. As a young child, he liked the Dr. Seuss books. Later, he started reading biographies and war stories. One reason why he feels lucky to be an illustrator is because he can listen to books on tape while he works. Mike is available to provide custom illustrations for all manner of publications at reasonable prices. Mike can be reached at **www.mikereedillustration.com**.

The Oracle In-Focus Series

The *Oracle In-Focus* series is a unique publishing paradigm, targeted at Oracle professionals who need fast and accurate working examples of complex issues. *Oracle In-Focus* books are unique because they have a super-tight focus and quickly provide Oracle professionals with what they need to solve their problems.

Oracle In-Focus books are designed for the practicing Oracle professional. Oracle In-Focus books are an affordable way for all Oracle professionals to get the information they need, and get it fast.

Expert Authors – All *Oracle In-Focus* authors are content experts and are carefully screened for technical ability and communications skills.

Online Code Depot – All code scripts from *Oracle In-Focus* books are available on the web for instant download. Those who purchase a book will get the URL and password to download their scripts.

Lots of working examples – *Oracle In-Focus* is packed with working examples and pragmatic tips.

No theory – Practicing Oracle professionals know the concepts they need, working code to get started fast.

Concise – Most *Oracle In-Focus* books are less than 200 pages and get right to-the-point of the tough technical issues.

Tight focus - The *Oracle In-Focus* series addresses tight topics and targets specific technical areas of Oracle technology.

Affordable – Reasonably priced, *Oracle In-Focus* books are the perfect solution to challenging technical issues.

http://www.Rampant-Books.com

Conducting the UNIX Job Interview

IT Manager Guide with UNIX Interview Questions

Adam Haeder

ISBN 0-9744355-6-2

Retail Price $16.95 / £10.95

This book is the accumulated observations of the authors' interviews with hundreds of job candidates. The author provides useful insights into what characteristics make a good UNIX programmer and offer their accumulated techniques as an aid to interviewing an UNIX job candidate.

This handy guide has a complete set of UNIX job interview questions and provides a complete method for accurately accessing the technical abilities of UNIX job candidates. By using UNIX job interview questions that only an experienced person knows, your supervisor can ask the right interview questions and fill your UNIX job with the best qualified UNIX developer.

- Assists the IT manager in choosing the best-qualified UNIX professionals.

- Provides proven techniques that can accurately ascertain a job candidate's suitability for an UNIX position.

www.Rampant-Books.com

Free!
Oracle 10g Senior DBA Reference Poster

This 24 x 36 inch quick reference includes the important data columns and relationships between the DBA views, allowing you to quickly write complex data dictionary queries.

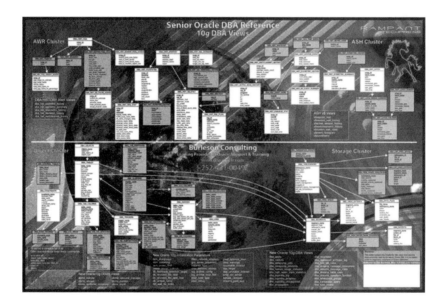

This comprehensive data dictionary reference contains the most important columns from the most important Oracle10g DBA views. Especially useful are the Automated Workload Repository (AWR) and Active Session History (ASH) DBA views.

WARNING - This poster is not suitable for beginners. It is designed for senior Oracle DBAs and required knowledge of Oracle data dictionary internal structures. You can get your poster at this URL:

www.rampant.cc/postcr.htm